UNDERCURRENTS   Series Editor Carol Coulter

The Politics of Children's Rights

FRANK MARTIN

CORK UNIVERSITY PRESS

First published in 2000 by
Cork University Press
University College
Cork
Ireland

© Frank Martin 2000

British Library Cataloguing in Publication Data
A CIP catalogue record for this book is available from
the British Library

ISBN 1 85918 272 0

Typeset by Tower Books, Ballincollig, Co. Cork
Printed by Colour Books Ltd., Baldoyle, Dublin

Contents

Acknowledgements

I wish to thank Carol Coulter, series editor, for her incisive comments on earlier drafts of this *Undercurrents* text. Thanks are also due to the staff of Cork University Press for their professional efficiency.

I would also like to express my gatitude to my colleagues in the Department of Law UCC for their advice and support.

I have endeavoured to state the law as of 16 October 2000.

Frank Martin,
16.10.2000

Abbreviations

AG	Attorney General
CFLQ	*Child and Family Law Quarterly*
CPA	Combat Poverty Agency
CRA	Children's Rights Alliance
DPP	Director of Public Prosecution
Fam LJ	*Family Law Journal*
FLR	*Family Law Reports*
GAL	Guardian *ad litem*
HC	High Court
IJFL	*Irish Journal of Family Law*
ILRM	*Irish Law Reports Monthly*
IR	*Irish Reports*
LRC	Law Reform Commission
NCS	National Children's Strategy
NGO	Non-Governmental Organisation
SC	Supreme Court
UN	United Nations
UNCRC	United Nations Convention on the Rights of the Child 1989
UNREP	Unreported

Table of Statutes

Adoption Acts 1952-1998
Child Abduction and Enforcement of Custody Orders
    Act 1991
Child Care Act 1991
Children Act 1997
Domestic Violence Act 1996
Education Act 1998
Family Law Act 1995
Family Law (Divorce) Act 1996
Family Law (Maintenance of Spouses and Children)
    Act 1976
Guardianship of Infants Act 1964
Non-Fatal Offences Against the Person Act 1997
Protection for Persons Reporting Child Abuse Act 1998
Registration of Births Acts 1863-1996
Status of Children Act 1987
Succession Act 1965

Table of International Conventions

Table of Cases

Introduction

Practitioners and policy makers are more concerned with
what rights children have or should have, than whether they
have rights at all. Their concerns are with balancing one
right against another in order to clarify measures for their
enforcement. But on a more theoretical level, there has been
a measure of speculation over whether children can be
termed rights-holders at all.

Jane Fortin[1]

In Irish society, children are a voiceless and very vulnerable
though significant minority group possessing few political or
legal powers. They do not have the right to vote. They are unable
to exert influence on any of the powerful lobbies and institutions
that inform and underpin political, social and economic change.
In terms of their right to have a certain degree of individual
autonomy, there has been a noticeable but gradual shift of
emphasis from pigeonholing children as commodities or
appendages of their parents or guardians. In the current political
climate there is evidence of socio-legal, structural and functional
developments, which have as their objective to highlight and
promote children's full capacity as human beings and citizens as
they make their inexorable way towards adulthood.

Both nationally and internationally, there is an on-going
debate about the nature and scope of children's rights. In
contemporary Ireland there is some evidence of progress in
implementing 'child-proofing' of policies and practices, which
may impact on children's lives as they negotiate their complex
passage towards full autonomy as adults. Any inclusion of children within the broad political dialogue must inevitably
contribute towards the greater democratisation of Irish society.
By proactively establishing an ethos which fosters the advancement of children's rights, Irish society would send out the
clearest unequivocal message that Irish children and young
people have a central and pivotal place in our evolving society
both as present and future citizens. This accentuation and eleva-
tion of children's rights and entitlements should not however be

interpreted as a threat to the traditional absolute authority of a parent/guardian, resulting in a partial or complete diminution of parental or familial rights. The essential thrust of a children's rights perspective is to establish, at a minimum, some bench- mark or threshold level, below which the lawmakers and policy makers cannot go. Some advocates of children's rights would regard the threshold approach as too low a standard. Others would be quite alarmed that society would even consider ascrib- ing to this minority a cluster of rights, duties and obligations endangering not only the democratic balance in Irish society but potentially jeopardising the delicate socio-legal balance which exists within the family unit.

It is sometimes stated that respect for human rights on a national level begins with the way a society as a whole cares for its children. Indeed the way a society treats children reflects not only its qualities of compassion and protective caring but also its sense of justice, its commitment to the future and its desire to enhance the human condition for coming generations.[2] The history of the Irish State's concern for children's issues has not been a distinguished one though things are beginning to change slowly but inexorably. Mere lip service to children's rights and duties is no longer acceptable. Children are now entitled to be seen *and* heard: as a public policy issue, the 'children' issue now matters. The Irish Courts, the United Nations Committee on the Rights of the Child and various non-governmental organisations as well as other pressure groups have all been responsible one way or another for moving children's rights up the political agenda.

The Irish Government can no longer afford to turn its back and ignore the whole issue of children's rights. The 'Celtic Tiger' must look after its young. The new millennium must be one of hope for all Irish children. It is time to consolidate all the disparate and fragmented developments concerning children that have taken place to date and develop a more coherent policy-driven approach towards establishing and enforcing rights. Merely declaring those rights to exist will no longer suffice; effective enforcement of those rights is essential. Therefore children's rights will need to be better resourced if these rights are to be actualised.

All children – whether healthy children or 'disturbed' – have rights. They have a right not to be hungry and not to suffer the ill-effects of poverty. They have rights to proper housing so that they can have the capacity to enjoy their childhood in a suitably civilised environment. The problem of 'homeless children' is surely concrete evidence that certain categories of children are not having their rights vindicated. They have rights to be fed physiologically and intellectually. They have the right to life but not a life that is characterised by malnutrition, abuse and neglect. They have rights to their bodily integrity and therefore should not be bullied at home, in recreational activities or in school. They should also not be physically or psychologically humiliated by parent, guardian or custodian within the family home. On a more controversial note, a right to bodily integrity might also entail teenagers having access to contraception. Bodily integrity rights of children would also imply that, within the criminal law context, children who breach the criminal codes do not belong in the criminal courts nor do they belong in the prisons. Indeed the Irish High Court has recently had to deal with the problem of the legal rights of 'disturbed' children, and what is most remarkable about the whole episode is the relentless opposition from various government departments to the judge-made creation of legal rights for those disturbed children. Nevertheless the High Court has continued, regardless of the accusation of offending the Separation of Powers Doctrine, to vindicate the rights of those children.

In Ireland, the legislature has been reasonably interventionist and proactive in both private and public child law matters. From the Child Care Act 1991 to the Children Act 1997 there have been concerted efforts to both establish and prioritise rights and responsibilities towards children. During the 1990s there has also been a plethora of other family legislation, all of which has indirect and/or direct implications for children. This additional development of child law has ensured, where practicable, that children as 'rights-bearing citizens' are entitled to be provided with a conflict-free milieu during their formative years as they make their way from birth to voting age. The Adoption Acts between 1988 and 1998 have updated the law regulating the adoption of marital and non-marital children as well as facilitating inter-country adoption. The Family Law Act 1995 gives certain legal, financial and relationship rights to children whose parents are seeking a decree of Judicial Separation. The Domestic Violence Act 1996 expressly protects children whose 'safety and welfare' are in danger within the familial context. The Family Law (Divorce) Act 1996, gives unequivocal financial and relationship rights to children whose parents are applying for a divorce decree. Indeed both Article 41.3.2. (iii) of the Irish Constitution and the 1996 Divorce Act stipulate that before granting a divorce decree the court must be satisfied that proper provision has been made for the children/dependent members of the family. The position of children therefore in divorce proceedings is central and failure by the divorcing spouses to provide for their children could result in the Family Court refusing the divorce decree application. Children are not entitled to be legally represented via their own lawyer to either oppose or support their parents' divorce application. For many Irish people this notion of autonomous rights for children in their parents' divorce action is a step too far even in this enlightened new millennium. Unlike in the USA, there have been no instances in Ireland where children have taken cases against their parents seeking to get a 'divorce' from them. The idea is a serious one, though it is often discussed somewhat flippantly. For example, the following questions merit consideration: Why should children be compelled to live in a familial environment in which they are permanently unhappy and unfulfilled? Ought they not to have some right to exit from this context via a formal 'divorce' from their parents? Before such a scenario becomes a reality, constitutional obstacles would have to be removed which would entail minimising the near absolute authority of the parent in Irish constitutional law vis-à-vis their child.

Although the 1989 United Nations Convention on the Rights of the Child (UNCRC) may not be the last word on children's rights, its norms are an acknowledged and accepted reference point for lawmakers both parliamentary and judicial. Some advocates of children's rights regard it as a Bill of Rights for children. Article 1 of the UNCRC states that the Convention applies 'to every human being below the age of eighteen years unless, under the law applicable to the child, a majority is attained earlier'. This is a chronological definition of a child and as such is an objective definition. To search for an alternative definition of a child based on a qualitative assessment of its relative maturity is much more problematic. Children should therefore have distinct rights from the moment of birth until age eighteen. However, along that chronological spectrum children as adolescents or as 'near adults' must surely, as a matter of law and common sense, have nearly all the rights that adults possess. The empowerment of children as fully autonomous human beings with legal rights and with ability to participate fully in Irish society must therefore be the new millennium challenge. Not only must lawmakers tackle this challenge but Irish society must begin to accept an evolving 'child liberation philosophy' which will improve the lives of children. Children can no longer be content with being treated as second-class citizens. Instead there must be an acceptance of the idea that children are rights-bearing citizens of their country and of the world. This objective will require the empowering of children to live their childhood with the maximum of equal opportunities.

Children of asylum-seekers/refugees and other immigrants also have legal rights in Irish society whether or not they are citizens of this State. Immigration to Ireland is a novel situation for most Irish people who must now become accustomed to the idea that a multi-ethnic Ireland brings with it major responsibilities towards the children of other ethnic groups. Paul Cullen assesses the situation as follows: 'The arrival of about 10,000 asylum-seekers into Ireland over the past five years has had a massive impact on Irish life, far out of proportion to the numbers involved.'[3] Child refugees or children of refugees as a discrete group are doubly vulnerable, both as children and as refugees. Children who have been born in Ireland of parents who are refugees/asylum-seekers automatically acquire Irish citizenship and are entitled to an Irish passport, which is in effect a European passport. These children also, on birth, acquire automatic constitutional rights, one of which includes the right to the society of their parents until they reach the age of majority. Their parents therefore have a near automatic right of residence in Ireland if their child is born here. The Department of Justice revealed in June 2000 that, between January 1999 and April 2000, permission had been granted to 1,413 asylum-seekers to remain in Ireland on the basis that they were now parents of an Irish-born child. Births to asylum seekers/refugees have increased five-fold compared to last year at the National Maternity Hospital Dublin. The Master of the Rotunda Hospital Dublin, Dr McKenna, stated in June 2000 that if the trend continued, the hospital would deliver 700 non-nationals/asylum-seekers by the end of 2000, twice the number delivered in 1998. Over 100 child refugees are in Ireland on the basis of their own independent refugee status since they have no adult to care for them. These children arrived in Ireland unaccompanied by parents or other adults with responsibility for their welfare. At present, Ireland has obligations to all these children under Article 22 of the UNCRC, which states that:

> State Parties shall take appropriate measures to ensure that a child who is seeking refugee status or who is considered a refugee . . . shall whether unaccompanied or accompanied . . . receive appropriate protection and humanitarian assistance in the enjoyment of applicable rights.[4]

The Irish Government must now begin to develop a more cogent child refugee policy in order to comply with international and national legal obligations in terms of provision of the education, housing and welfare needs of these children. The human rights of all children in Ireland, citizens and non-citizens must now be respected equally. Respect for human rights begins with the way a society as a whole cares for all its children.

This book therefore describes and analyses the nature and scope of children's legal rights within various contexts in the Republic of Ireland, and seeks to establish whether they are more honoured in the breach than in the observance. Inculcating a culture of respect for children's rights within a democratic society is a slow and complex process. Bestowing on children, as a discrete group, fundamental rights of autonomy and self-determination could sound alarm bells in Irish society generally and more particularly within the family sphere. By ascribing rights to children where previously there were few, the peculiar balance between individual members within the family unit may be radically altered. The challenge of finding the right balance must be met as the twenty-first century progresses.

1. The International Context

Children's rights have moved from the margins of discussion to centre stage. The 1989 UNCRC is the most rapidly and universally accepted human rights document of the century . . . The UNCRC is striking evidence of a major twentieth-century revolution in how we conceptualise children's law.
Professor Woodhouse[5]

The twentieth of November 1999 marked the tenth anniversary of the acceptance by the United Nations of the Convention on the Rights of the Child (UNCRC).[6] By 1998, 191 State Parties had either acceded to or ratified the Convention. The USA and Somalia are the only two states not to have ratified it. Professor

Michael Freeman, an acknowledged family law scholar, has suggested that perhaps too many States ratified the Convention 'without giving serious thought to their own domestic laws and practices and to what would be entailed in ratifying the Convention'.[7] A rapid ratification is one thing but giving substance to the Convention is another. It is readily acknowledged that no other international treaty has achieved such a level of consensus or been responded to so rapidly by so many even though it may not be the definitive text on children's rights. The Republic of Ireland ratified the UNCRC on 21 September 1992 and it came into force on 21 October 1992. By ratifying the Convention, Ireland confirmed its complete acceptance of domestic and international obligations to children according to the key minimum threshold standards embodied in the Convention. The degree of a State Party's implementation of and compliance with the UNCRC is monitored and evaluated by means of a formal reporting process undertaken by a specially designated UN Committee on the Rights of the Child.

In January 1998 in Geneva, the Irish Government's 136-page Compliance Report was officially scrutinised by the UN Committee on the Rights of the Child. The Department of Foreign Affairs is the Government Department with primary responsibility for co-ordinating human rights issues in Ireland. Their brief also includes children's rights. Accordingly the Department of Foreign Affairs was the principal drafter of the Irish Compliance Report submitted to the UN Committee. *The Concluding Observations of the UN Committee* (1998) were severely critical of the Republic of Ireland's less than enthusiastic endeavours in promoting and prioritising children's rights.[8] The Committee's *Observations* do not, nor are they intended to, address individual children's problems within the private sphere of the family, since the Convention is primarily directed at the public functions of states and not at parents as they live their family lives within the family home.

In relation to their comments on Ireland, the primary focus was on governmental policies on a broad spectrum of issues such as:

- children's education in Ireland
- children with disabilities
- corporal punishment in schools and in the home
- counselling services
- juvenile justice
- homelessness
- child-begging
- breastfeeding

Strong words were used in the UN's *Observations* report about the absence or inadequacy of Irish governmental policies and programmes which regulated those eight areas associated directly or indirectly with children living in Ireland.

Ireland's ratification of the UNCRC was without any reservations or declarations. In contrast, the United Kingdom entered six reservations on ratifying the Convention in December 1991. Ireland's ratification could have occurred sooner but the Irish Government wanted to have a significant body of child law in place prior to ratification in order to accommodate the key principles of the Convention. The Child Care Act 1991 mirrors fairly closely the Convention's maxims regarding children's protection rights from neglect, ill-treatment and abuse as well as children's rights to proper standards of child care. Some of the hallmarks of the Child Care Act 1991 are its express aim, firstly to ensure that the *best interest of the child* is a primary consideration and secondly, that the child's right to have due consideration given to its wishes is unequivocally protected.[9] Article 3 (1) of the UNCRC and Sections 3 and 24 of the Child Care Act 1991 address the welfare principle as it applies to child law:

> In all actions concerning children, whether undertaken by public or private social welfare institutions, courts of law, administrative authorities or legislative bodies, the best interests of the child shall be a primary consideration.

Sections 3 and 24 of the Child Care Act 1991 stipulate that in their respective functions and proceedings, Health Boards and Courts 'shall regard the welfare of the child as the first and paramount consideration'. At first glance this seems to be an unambiguous and clear guarantee to children that their welfare is the State's primary concern. However, the seeming absoluteness of this unequivocal provision is quickly qualified in Section 25 of the Child Care Act 1991 with the proviso that the 'welfare principle' is applied to child care proceedings 'having regard to the rights and duties of parents, whether under the Constitution or otherwise'. Thus parental rights and authority over their children continue to be privileged. Of equal significance is the marked similarity between Article 12 of the UNCRC and Sections 3, 24 and 25 of the Child Care Act 1991 which address the controversial issue of prioritising the principle of the 'views of the child' being accorded a degree of importance. Article 12 states that:

> State Parties shall assure to the child who is capable of forming his or her own views the right to express those views freely in all matters affecting the child, the *views of the child* being given due weight in accordance with the age and maturity of the child [my emphasis] .

The Child Care Act 1991 also requires Health Boards and Courts in their respective functions and proceedings 'in so far as is practicable [to] give due consideration to the wishes of the child'. Ireland's *First National Compliance Report* (1996) to the UN Committee on the Rights of the Child vigorously defended the proactive nature of this domestic child law as being in harmony with the Convention's requirements. The Irish Government's *Compliance Report* optimistically stated that:

> The Child Care Act represents a movement away from the concept of children as parental property to an understanding of the child as a person who has rights by virtue of being a child. It is one of the most enlightened pieces of legislation enacted in recent years and updated all earlier legislation to take account of situations of neglect and abuse . . . [10]

The UN Committee's evaluation of the 1991 Child Care Act's scope and philosophy was, however, much more qualified and restrained and indeed was quite critical of the absence of a consistent children's rights approach in the Act. Nevertheless, the UN Committee welcomed 'the enactment of the Child Care Act 1991 and its various amendments since then, including the Children Act 1997, thereby reinforcing the status of the child as a full subject of rights'.[11] Ireland clearly then ratified the UN Convention only after giving serious consideration to the ramifications for Irish child law. Since the early 1990s, Irish children are beginning to be recognised and treated as juristic persons with a special status requiring special care and protection.

The UNCRC is now regarded as a landmark legal instrument dealing with Family/Child Law with the express objective of enhancing the position of children and young people as 'rights owners'. However, critics of the UNCRC argue that it may be an unnecessary convention as there are already in existence many international conventions dealing with the fundamental rights of all human beings which inevitably must include children within the class of persons in need of protection. Indeed, the Convention represents a virtually universal acceptance of the idea that children are rights-bearing citizens of their countries and of the world.[12] The Convention also treats the child as a juristic person. According to a UNICEF Report (1990) the Convention is:

> an ideal which few nations have so far achieved but implicit in the tissues and sinews of the Convention's tenets is the hope that it will gradually become the standard below which any nation, rich or poor, would be too ashamed to fall.[13]

The Convention also acknowledges the primacy of the family, but, in the event of family breakdown or dysfunction, it stipulates that the State may provide a form of alternative care. The type of care will depend on the particular political and ideological circumstances of each State Party to the UNCRC. The fifty-four Articles of the Convention represent the grand design for promoting the globalisation of children's rights incorporating what Andrew Bainham classifies as the '4 Ps':

- Prevention,
- Protection,
- Provision and
- Participation.[14]

In addition, the Convention has achieved a significant level of consensus among many nations (including Ireland) on complex and controversial child-related issues, a consensus which was previously thought to be impossible. In ideological and practical terms the Convention is primarily concerned with rights rather than with paternalistic attitudes to children's welfare. One major and influential academic study, which addresses the unique international legal status of children, concludes with the assertion that children are not to be regarded as 'miniature adults' and insists that:

> Children are not adults in miniature. They are beings *per se*, different from their elders in their mental nature, their functioning, their understanding of events, and their reactions to them. This effort to highlight the differences between adult and child, however, should not obscure the enormous variations in the quality and degree of such differences not only among different children but also in each individual child during the fluctuating course of his growth and development as a member of a family.[15]

Of necessity, recognition and advancement of children's rights inevitably entail, according to a liberal perspective, a limitation of what is termed 'family autonomy'. This potential for intrusion into and abridgement of 'family autonomy' has particular problems for Ireland, which has a written Constitution containing a complete Article (Article 41) devoted to 'The Family', which guarantees *inter alia* to protect its authority from unjust attacks by the

State. American opponents of the UNCRC, supported by right-wing fundamentalist religious groups, highlight the abridgement argument as the Achilles heel of the Convention by comparing the Convention to a blank cheque for government intervention within the home. Other critics also suggest that the UNCRC was primarily drafted merely with a view to eliminating Third World child abuse practices, no more and no less. According to S. Kilbourne, Director of Research, Child Rights International Research Institute, London, these negative interpretations are based on distorted readings of the Convention's various Articles.[16] She also notes that the UNCRC is:

> . . . intended to set standards for Governmental policies regarding children. It is a policy framework, not a code of parental conduct. The Convention does not provide for investigation or persecution against parents or guardians. In fact, no form of the word 'prosecute' appears anywhere in the Convention. Rather it is intended to be implemented through governmental programmes and policies. The civil and political rights such as freedoms of expression, religion and association, and the right to privacy, are protection from *governmental* intrusions – not parental guidance.

It is true that children's fundamental civil, social, economic, political, recreational and cultural rights are technically unenforceable by individual children in the courts, particularly where the UNCRC has not been expressly incorporated into domestic law. Incorporation of the UNCRC into each State's domestic laws, including Ireland's, has not been uniform. In precisely the same manner as the United Kingdom, ratification by Ireland of the UN Convention did not imply that its substantive provisions were automatically to form an influential or indeed any part of domestic law. To have that status and effect, it would have been necessary to incorporate formally the UN Convention into Irish law. In Ireland such incorporation has not occurred due to certain Constitutional constraints and difficulties.

Although the Irish Government is entitled to ratify international treaties or agreements, such powers are severely limited under Article 29.6 of the 1937 Irish Constitution which states that: 'No international agreement shall be part of the domestic law of the State save as may be determined by the *Oireachtas.*' In effect this has meant that the UNCRC is binding on the Irish State only to the extent that Ireland is under a moral obligation under international law principles to ensure that the Articles and terms are honoured in the spirit and the letter of the law. To date, the Irish Parliament has declined to incorporate the entire UNCRC into Irish law because of potential incongruity and unconstitutionality of several controversial provisions with the Irish Constitution, in particular Article 41. This Article expressly acknowledges the authority and autonomy of parents *vis-à-vis* their children. Ironically the word 'child' is used only once in the Irish Constitution and then only within the context of Article 42 which deals with education rights.[17] However, this does not mean that the Republic of Ireland has never incorporated an international treaty, dealing with children, into domestic law.

In order to tackle the international transjurisdictional problem of parental child abduction, Ireland has ratified and subsequently incorporated two international conventions into Irish law – The Hague Convention on the Civil Aspects of International Child Abduction signed on 25 October 1980 at The Hague Conference on Private International Law (Hague Convention), and the Council of Europe's Convention on Recognition and Enforcement of Decisions Concerning Custody of Children and on Restoration of Custody of Children, signed at Luxembourg on 20 May 1980 (Luxembourg Convention). On 1 October 1991 both Conventions were expressly incorporated and now have force of law through the Child Abduction and Enforcement of Custody Orders Act 1991. Part II of the Act gives direct and immediate effect to the Hague Convention, while Part III gives effect to the Luxembourg Convention. Along with the UK and USA, Ireland is acknowledged as a country which strictly adheres to the principles of both Conventions on child abduction. Justice

Keane in *Wadda v Ireland* (1994), summarised the underlying child-centred policy of the Conventions when he stated that:

> Their underlying purpose is to ensure stability for children, by putting a brisk end to the efforts of parents to have their children's future decided where they want and when they want, by removing them from their country of residence to another jurisdiction chosen arbitrarily by the absconding parent.

Indeed, at the time of writing the Irish Parliament is at the second stage in processing additional legislation for incorporating further international children's human rights law. The Protection of Children (Hague Convention) Bill 1998 incorporates the Hague Convention of 19 October 1996 on Jurisdiction, Applicable Law, Recognition, Enforcement and Co-operation in Respect of Parental Responsibility and Measures for the Protection of Children. If the proposed legislation is passed it will enable Ireland to formally ratify the 1996 Hague Convention, which aims to develop inter-State co-operation on custody disputes concerning children. It also contains measures for locating missing children, measures for protecting a child's property, and powers for a child's representative to act abroad. The Convention seeks to determine which authorities have jurisdiction to take measures directed towards protection of the person or property of a child. It will also determine which law is to be applied by such authorities in exercising their jurisdiction. This Protection of Children Bill also provides for the recognition and enforcement of such measures of protection in all contracting States. According to William Duncan, First Secretary, Hague Conference on Private International Law:

> The prospects for the Convention appear encouraging. One State, Monaco, has ratified it and two, the Netherlands and Morocco, have signed it. Preparations are in train for implementation in a number of other States, including the Republic of Ireland and the Netherlands,

and the signals from yet others such as the United Kingdom, Australia and the United States are positive.[18]

Enforceability of the 1989 UNCRC is probably contingent on the degree of public scrutiny which the UN Committee on the Rights of the Child gives to a particular State's compliance report and the subsequent publicity that may arise as a consequence of the Committee's negative evaluation of a report. The detailed scrutiny of Ireland's Compliance Report led to a lot of adverse publicity in Ireland's national media which provoked a great deal of defensive utterances from government ministers and civil service personnel. At the core of the enforceability debate is the fact that since children's so-called rights are progressive in nature then it follows, as Bainham has realistically noted, that 'ultimate enforceability is dependent on political will and the availability and massive commitment of resources in individual countries'.[19] According to the UN Committee, Ireland may have had the political will, but fragmentation of efforts was the distinguishing hallmark of the Irish Government's approach towards child policy.

2. Non-Governmental Organisations and Children's Rights

The protection of the international rights of the child . . . depends on resources, which are not a matter of international law but of international political will. Political will can be increased if the successes of child rights are highlighted.
                                         Van Bueren.[20]

In Ireland there are many non-governmental organisations which have as their objective the establishment, advancement and protection of children's rights. Opinions vary significantly as to the role and value of such organisations, particularly their direct or indirect, formal and informal involvement in the various stages of the UN reporting process. The UN Committee on the Rights of the Child has tended to rely on NGOs' documentary and oral submissions in order to get a fuller, more reliable, less partisan perspective on a State's degree of compliance. Some State Parties regard this NGO intervention as undesirable, as NGOs are considered to be zealous and idealistic as well as altruistic interlopers. In Ireland one of the main child-related NGOs is the Children's Rights Alliance (CRA), which is a national umbrella group with sixty member organisations, including a wide range of child welfare agencies, youth representative groups, parent organisations, unions and professional associations representing those working with children and others with a commitment to children's rights. The CRA was set up in 1993 to promote awareness of the UNCRC in Ireland and to seek its implementation through the reform and improvement of legislation, policies and services. According to the Children's Right Alliance:

> Ireland's ratification of the UNCRC and the formation of the Children's Rights Alliance have provided groups with concern and responsibility for children with an opportunity to work together more effectively . . . Relationships are weak between governmental and non-governmental sectors with regard to the formulation and implementation of policy to meet children's needs . . . There is a need to put formal structures in place to enable positive, collaborative relationships to develop with and between government and non-governmental sectors thereby facilitating the implementation of the UN Convention in Ireland.[21]

Without doubt the 1989 UNCRC gave the CRA a structured focus for their children's rights campaign. Fragmentation of earlier CRA efforts was replaced by a more confident, reorganised, well-funded and centralised nationwide organisation, which was well informed through the utilisation of academic researchers from the area of child policy and child law areas. It is readily acknowledged that the CRA contributed significantly to the UN Committee's overall and complete understanding of Ireland's actual, as opposed to their aspirational, degree of compliance with the tenets and principles of the UNCRC.

In drafting the Irish Government's Compliance Report, the Department of Foreign Affairs consulted with a representative cross-section of the NGO sector interested in children's welfare. This consultation process facilitated meaningful presentation of alternative perspectives, thus ensuring an accurate and comprehensive reflection of the qualitative status of Ireland's implementation of the UNCRC. The Department's view about the precise status of those consultations was that 'the meetings did not set out to achieve agreement or consensus but rather allowed constructive dialogue and exchange of views on the report under the standard eight headings adopted by the UN Committee'.[22] The Children's Rights Alliance subsequently consolidated its views as outlined in its publication, *Small Voices: Vital Rights*,[23] which represented its formal submission to the UNCRC. Indeed it seems that the protracted reporting process necessitated and encouraged interaction between civil servants, government officials and other elements in Irish civil society as a democratic expression of public participation in the scrutiny of child-related government policies. However, on the issue of a co-ordinated collaborative relationship between governmental and non-governmental sectors on children's rights, the CRA noted that:

> Policy decisions are often taken by statutory authorities with little or no involvement from the NGO sector. Any involvement which does occur results more often from lobbying by NGOs than from invitation by statutory authorities . . . However there is a need to put formal structures in place to enable positive collaborative relationships to develop with and between government and non-governmental sectors thereby facilitating the implementation of the UN Convention in Ireland.

Capitalising on the potential of this monitoring process for maximising an NGO's opportunity to criticise their State Party's compliance levels, the Irish NGOs itemised unequivocally the lacunae, inadequacies and inaccuracies in the Report.[24] The NGOs called for significant amendments to the Irish Constitution in order to expressly expand and protect the constitutional guarantees for children's rights. In particular, they referred to various constitutional problems associated with children's rights in Ireland, especially Article 41 of the Irish Constitution which does not expressly contain specific enumerated rights for children. The NGOs have repeatedly called for constitutional amendments that would codify and incorporate any judicially discovered and recognised implied constitutional rights into an expanded version of Article 41. In Ireland the judiciary has been creative and innovative in establishing and expanding the rights portfolio of children. The contribution of the judiciary will be examined in the next section.

3. Children's Rights in Irish Courts: 1980–2000

The idea that parents' rights necessarily diminish in scope and strength as the child grows older and moves towards independence has not been explored in Irish constitutional law. The potential for development of such a doctrine exists but has been little exploited. It is ironic that the very powerlessness of children has deprived them of the means to assert in the courts any independent constitutional status.

William Duncan[25]

Since the 1980s, the Irish High Court and Supreme Court have had to become interpretively creative in order to 'discover' unenumerated children's rights within the penumbra of the text of the Irish Constitution. This has resulted in an expansion of various constitutional guarantees for the substance and scope of the rights of the child in Ireland. Although Article 41 of the Irish Constitution contains the main provisions relating to the Family, its focus is on the rights of the Family as a distinct social *unit* with an emphasis on protecting it from intervention by the State rather than on the rights of the individual members of the Family. Only Article 42.5, which is entitled 'Education', makes the one specific reference to 'the natural and imprescriptible rights of the child' by stating that:

> In exceptional cases, where the parents for physical or moral reasons fail in the duty towards their children, the State as guardian of the common good, by appropriate means shall endeavour to supply the place of the parents, but always with due regard for the natural and imprescriptible rights of the child.

One of the earliest commitments in twentieth-century Irish politics to asserting children's rights was contained in the 1916 Proclamation. This document, which was issued by the Provisional Government during the Rebellion against Britain, proclaimed the Irish Republic. On children's rights it stated: 'The Republic guarantees religious and civil liberty, equal rights and equal opportunities to all its citizens and declares its resolve to pursue the happiness and prosperity of the whole nation and of all its parts, cherishing all the *children* of the nation equally . . .' [my emphasis]

In *WO'R v. EH (Guardianship)* (1996), Justice Barrington in the Supreme Court gave some judicial clarification to the interplay (if any) of the respective constitutional rights of the various units within the family context. He also examined the interconnectedness between two Articles of the Irish Constitution, which make direct and indirect references to children's rights. At the statutory level Justice Barrington also expanded on the hitherto uncertain legal ambit and legal weight to be attached to the child's welfare principle. For Justice Barrington J, Article 42 of the Constitution is:

> an extension of Article 41 and refers to parents and children within the family context. It refers to the inalienable rights and duties of parents and to the imprescriptible rights of the child. In other words, it refers to a relationship between three people which carries with it reciprocal rights and duties which the positive law is enjoined to respect. The rights of the child are clearly predominant. They alone are described as being

> imprescriptible but the parents also have rights . . . the welfare[26] of the child is to be the most important consideration but that this is not the only consideration. Otherwise the drafters of the Guardianship of Infants 1964 Act would not have chosen the 'adjective' first.[27]

The Guardianship of Infants Act 1964 is the principal legislation regulating most child-related private law proceedings and was primarily responsible for the establishment of the benchmark principle of the 'paramount welfare of the child' in such proceedings. To date this paramountcy principle has remained constant throughout all child-related legislation. Implied children's constitutional rights – such as the right to bodily integrity and the right to an opportunity to be reared with due regard to religious, moral, intellectual and physical welfare – were identified by the Irish Supreme Court in *G v. An Bord Uchtála (The Adoption Board)* (1980). Further additional elaborations to the list of children's rights were made by the then Chief Justice O'Higgins who stated that a born child had a right:

> . . . to be fed and to live, to be reared and educated and to have the opportunity of working and realising his or her full personality and dignity as a human being. These rights of the child (and others, which I have not enumerated) must equally be protected and vindicated by the State.

Justice Brian Walsh, another Supreme Court Judge in the same case, also stated that the rights of the child must necessarily include the right:

> to rest and recreation, to the practice of religion, and to follow his or her conscience . . . the right to maintain one's life at a proper human standard in matters of food, clothing and habitation . . . The child's natural right to life and all that flows from that right are independent of any right of the parent as such.

In *FN (a minor) v. Minister for Education* (1995), Justice Geoghegan in the High Court, dealt with an application for a child care order under the Child Care Act 1991 for a child who suffered from a hyperkinetic disorder and thus required both containment and treatment so that his welfare might be attended to. He made a formal declaration that 'the State is under a constitutional obligation towards the applicant to establish as soon as reasonably practicable . . . suitable arrangements of containment with treatment for the applicant'. Justice Geoghegan made clear the State's constitutional obligation to FN. The State authorities could therefore have been in no doubt of their obligation in that regard as the judge did no more than make a declaration as to the entitlement of FN to the appropriate treatment. In a retrospective critique of this judgment some five years later Justice Kelly indicated in the case of *ST v. Minister for Health and Children* (2000) that:

> This [High Court] was entitled to expect that once appraised of the constitutional obligations owed to FN the State would take the necessary steps to have the matter remedied. Not merely was the Court entitled to have such an expectation but it was obliged to ensure that that expectation would be realised 'as soon as practicable'.

In *TM and AM v. An Bord Uchtála* (1998), Justice O'Flaherty stated in the Supreme Court that: 'The minimum requirements are that a child should have adequate shelter, food, clothing and care, including especially medical care, as well as a basic education. These requirements constitute the rights of the child and are surely of universal application.' In *DG v. Eastern Health Board* (1998), Justice Denham, also in the Supreme Court, held that a child has 'a right to equality, to the right of a good name and to the right of personal liberty'. In *A and B v. Eastern Health Board* (1998), Justice Geoghegan held that 'a thirteen-year-old pregnant girl has a constitutional right to a permissible termination of her pregnancy where there is a real and substantial risk to her life, as distinct from her health'. Other subsequent Irish superior court judgments have acknowledged the Irish State's obligation to cater for 'special needs' of children, particularly where the special needs cannot be provided by the parents or guardian.

In *Wadda v. Ireland* (1994), the Irish High Court examined the scope of children's constitutional rights under Private International Law principles, in particular those rights which apply exclusively within the context of parental transnational child abduction circumstances. The mother, an Irish citizen who was habitually resident with her husband (a Moroccan citizen) and child in the United Kingdom, removed the child to Ireland without the consent or acquiescence of the husband. The Irish High Court ordered the return of the child to the UK. By virtue of Section 6 (1) of the Child Abduction and Enforcement of Custody Orders Act 1991, The Hague Convention on the Civil Aspects of International Child Abduction (The Hague Convention) has force of law in Ireland. At issue was the argument (advanced by the abductor/mother) that a Hague Convention application under this Act of 1991 was unconstitutional given that it was merely a procedural summary process which generally excluded domestic courts from determining substantive questions relating to child custody and access. Far from violating children's rights, Justice Keane held that The Hague Convention, as incorporated, gave children a constitutional right to be 'protected from the harmful effects of their wrongful removal from the states of their habitual residence'. Furthermore, he noted that:

> the personal rights of children under the Constitution are fully protected and vindicated by the provisions of the [Hague] Convention . . . it affords them an additional machinery for the protection and vindication of their constitutional rights which was not hitherto available.[28]

The inadequacy of the status of children's implied constitutional rights was alluded to by Justice Catherine McGuinness in *Comerford v. Minister for Education* (1997), involving a dysfunctional family with an 'out of control' 11-year-old boy who had serious behavioural problems including attention deficit disorder. Justice McGuinness referred to 'the comparative lack of express constitutional rights for the child as against the parents, bearing in mind the extremely strong rights given to parents and the family in the Constitution'. In the *Kilkenny Incest Investigation Report* (1993) the investigation team, headed by Mrs Catherine McGuinness SC (as she then was), recommended a constitutional change in order to give some equilibrium of rights within the family unit. One central discussion in this Report was the precise effect Article 41 of the Irish Constitution has had on the interpretation of child law and the framing of legislation in regard to children. The Report stated that:

> While we accept that the courts have on many occasions stressed that children are possessed of constitutional rights we are somewhat concerned that the *'natural and impresciptible rights of the child'* are specifically referred to in only one subarticle (Article 42.5) and then only in the context of the State supplying the place of parents who have failed in their duty. We feel that the very high emphasis on the rights of the family in the Constitution may consciously or unconsciously be interpreted as giving a higher value to the rights of parents than to the rights of children. We believe that the Constitution should contain a specific and overt declaration of the rights of born children. We therefore recommend that consideration be given by the Government to the amendment of Articles 41 and 42 of the Constitution so as to include a statement of the constitutional rights of children. We do not ourselves feel competent to put forward a particular wording and we suggest that study might be made of international documents such as the United Nations Convention of the Rights of the Child.[29]

The principles established by Justice Geoghegan in *FN v. Minister for Education* (1995) regarding the rights of special needs children were subsequently followed by Justice McGuinness in *Comerford v. The Minister for Education* (1997), as were the principles set out by Justice O'Hanlon J in *O'Donoghue v. Minister for Health* (1996).[30] This latter judgment resembles a children's rights charter for it contains an extensive and comprehensive survey of the various relevant authorities on children's rights in Irish and selected other common law jurisdictions. Also significant in Justice O'Hanlon's judgment is his reliance on the UNCRC as a source of law, which he suggests is more than a persuasive legal authority for courts. He further implied that the UNCRC is an essential guide for Irish courts in the area of children's rights. In a recent Supreme Court case, *TMM v. MD* (1999), which involved the transnational abduction of a child by a parent into Ireland, the Court confirmed that in the absence of court regulations in relation to the implementation of the Child Abduction and Enforcement of Custody Orders Act 1991, and in particular the Court's approach towards ascertaining the wishes of a child and the interview process and procedure, Article 12 of the UNCRC provided useful and relevant guidance. Since 1994 the New Zealand Family Courts are increasingly acknowledging the UNCRC and applying the purely due process legal rights which it grants. However, according to Pauline Tapp's research, 'New Zealand's Family Courts face a policy dilemma when asked to implement children's rights that impinge on political, economic, cultural and social work systems'.[31]

In the last two years, a cluster of case law has emerged from Irish Courts consolidating and elaborating the scope of children's constitutional rights, particularly within the context of deficiencies in child care services in Ireland. These cases take the form of an application to the courts for an injunction for something to be done for children. It seems that this is the only effective and successful method of remedying the plight of children needing immediate and necessary specialised and secure care. The High Court in *DB (a minor) v. Minister for Justice* (1999) was invited to go beyond an abstract consideration of children's rights and become 'involved in the enforcement of [children's] . . . constitutional rights in a much more direct way than has been the case heretofore'.[32] At issue was an 'out of control' child with special needs who was not provided with suitable arrangements of containment due to the Government's failure to fund the building of secure high-support units by the Health Boards. A High Court injunction was sought seeking to compel the State to provide resources to the Eastern Health Board to build, open and maintain those units. Justice Kelly noted the Minister for Health's failure 'to take timeous and effective steps to meet those needs', and indicated that there could be occasions and circumstances whereby it would be open to courts to become involved in 'matters of policy', particularly:

> if such intervention were required in order for this [High] Court to carry out its duties under the Constitution in securing, vindicating and enforcing constitutional rights [of children] . . . the time has now come for this Court to take the next step required of it under the Constitution so as to ensure that the rights of troubled minors who require placement of the type envisaged are met.[33]

Commenting on the legal ramifications of this particular case, Paul Ward has noted that:

> The State's inactivity in this regard is nothing short of disgraceful not simply to the children for whose welfare the State is constitutionally obliged to make provision for but also for the blatant disregard for the judiciary . . . The case is unique. Never before has a High Court been requested to direct the implementation of policy of the administrative branch of Government.[34]

Another example in which the Irish judiciary has assumed the pivotal role of champion and proactive guardian of children's rights arose in the public law sphere. The Eastern Health Board objected to the specific details of a District Judge's Child Care Order under the provisions of the Child Care Act 1991. The unusual aspect of the case was that a District Judge, on 26 December 1997, delivered a twelve-page reserved judgment giving specific directions to the Eastern Health Board that were incorporated into his Order. The parents of CK (the child) cohabited for some time but were not married and, at the time of the High Court hearing, were living apart. The application before the Court was one seeking to have CK committed to the care of the Health Board. In *Eastern Health Board v. District Judge JP McDonnell* (1999), a judicial review application, the Eastern Health Board objected to the lower Court's direction that:

   (i) the next Social Worker allocated to the child's (CK) case should not be a new recruit given the complexity of the case and;

   (ii) that CK not be sent for any therapy without prior reference by the Health Board to Dr Moran and the permission of the Court.

The Health Board argued that the District Judge's directions were *ultra vires* and secondly, that such judicial intervention could cause serious administrative problems, especially if more than one body were responsible for the detailed and day-to-day welfare of the child once the child was in care. The general significance of the case was that it gave some direction as to the general and particular role which both the Health Board and the District Court play in such public law proceedings. The judgment also gave guidance as to the precise demarcation between Courts and Health Boards in such child care proceedings. Justice McCracken dealt with this High Court judicial review application and concluded that he was obliged to interpret the statutes in light of the Constitution. Specifically he stated that:

> It is the function of the Courts, and not of local authorities or Health Boards, to ensure that the constitutional guarantees given to an individual are upheld. Therefore, where the welfare of a citizen, and in particular of a child who is in need, is concerned there would have to be very clear delegation of powers if the obligation is to be imposed upon somebody other than Courts.

According to Justice McCracken, section 24 of the Child Care Act 1991 copper-fastened the Court's function as protector of children's rights – an undelegatable function – particularly in child care proceedings whereby the Court 'shall have regard to the welfare of the child as the first and paramount consideration'. Additionally, Justice McCracken held that section 47 of the Child Care Act 1991, which states that 'Where a child is in the care of the Health Board, the District Court may, of its own motion or on an application of any person give such directions and make such order on any question affecting the welfare of the child as it thinks proper and may vary or discharge any such direction or order', gave the Court the express statutory power to make the ultimate decision on the matter. His interpretation of that particular part of the Act was that it was:

> an all-embracing and wide-ranging provision which is intended to extract ultimate care of a child who comes within the Act in the hands of the District Court.[35]

The decision of *EHB v. District Judge JP McDonnell* (1999), however, is not a licence for excessive judicial interference with a Health Board's 'day-to-day decisions'. In upholding constitutional rights of children in child care proceedings Irish courts are empowered only in limited circumstances when matters of concern are brought to the attention of the Court which could reasonably be considered adversely to affect the welfare of the child.[36] Paul Ward suggests that the District Court directions were clearly at odds with section 18 (Care Orders of the Child Care Act 1991) since this section specifically reserves to the Health Board for its discretion the very matters which were the subject of the direction.[37] It would seem that one of the implications of the judgment is that it is the Courts, and not Health Boards, which have the ultimate say regarding matters concerning children in care. On this point Ward concludes that:

> Such a position has obvious advantages and disadvantages in relation to securing the welfare of children in need of care by ensuring that an appropriate care plan is drawn up and implemented. The judicial fettering of

the Health Board's control over a child in its care adds another layer of administration for both the courts and the Health Boards which in itself can be counter-productive for all concerned.[38]

4. Irish Courts – Refuge of Last Resort for Children

The issue now is not one of establishing the principle of chil-dren's rights but of extending the range of situations where the language is perceived as legitimate.

J. Roche.[39]

Ever since his High Court judgment in *DG v. Eastern Health Board* (1997), Mr Justice Peter Kelly has become known for championing and privileging the legal rights of children who appear in his courts. *The Irish Times* (25 March 2000) described him as a judge 'waging a one-man crusade from the bench to get the Irish State to discharge its [constitutional] responsibilities to troubled chil-dren who fall foul of the law'. Many of his High Court cases/judgments involve the treatment of children, especially those most at risk, such as children who are suicidal, out of control, prostitutes, alcoholics, drug addicts and those displaying aggressive violent behaviour and anti-social personality disor-ders. What is unique about these child law judgments is that Irish policy on 'children-at-risk' is being primarily driven by a deter-mined and principled High Court judge whose judgments are solidly rooted in Irish constitutional law and therefore are binding on all, or ought to be, including the Legislature and the Executive.

In the early 1990s, judges in Dublin's Children's Court began to exhort solicitors and barristers to take children's cases to the High Court as a means of vindicating their young clients' consti-tutional rights in the absence of appropriate political responses to the children's urgent need for protection as they made their way to adulthood. The legal lacuna created by the State's failure to provide appropriate facilities necessitated an interventionist judicial response. In a recent consolidated judgment, *ST v. Minister for Education, AG and Eastern Health Board* (2000), Justice Kelly was again faced with the appalling and scandalous dilemma of revisiting the State's lethargic and fragmented efforts at providing high-support units for children-in-need. If the beginning of the new millennium has not been characterised by a political response to such urgently needed legal remedies, the judgment in *ST v. Minister for Health, Education and AG* has not only filled that vacuum, but has stated categorically that if children have rights then they must be vindicated by the Courts. In this and other instances, the Irish Courts have begun to operate as a 'refuge of last resort', by reason of the failure of the Legislature and the Executive. Justice Kelly concurred with Justice Lynch's Supreme Court statement in *DPP v. Best* (2000), that:

> Children have relied upon the rights which they have as persons and citizens pursuant to the provisions of the Constitution . . . the fact that such applicants are children means that they have added rights given to them by the Constitution for their well-being and protection during their minority

The net result of the case of *ST v. Minister for Health, Education and AG* is that a number of children have won injunctions against the State compelling it to build more than forty special care units for such children in seven Health Board areas outside the Eastern Health Board. The alternative for Justice Kelly was to send many at-risk children with no criminal conviction to State remand centres or to prison because of the lack of appropriate facilities. In the opinion of Justice Kelly there was an almost infinite number of circumstances which can result in the necessity for intervention by the State in some manifestation or another so as to protect the well-being of children. He also observed that some children are not adequately protected by their parents, whether due to indifference or fecklessness, a destructive family environment, external pressure or the child's own condition. The High Court held the Department of Health and Children ultimately culpable for the delays in assisting those children, declaring that:

> In some cases, as in the present, the statutory regime fails to protect the child in difficulty whereupon recourse to the courts is necessary . . . the presence of *bona fide* intentions count for little if results are not being achieved which go to address the rights of these young people in a timeous fashion.

Surprisingly, the State (i.e. Minister for Education, AG and the Eastern Health Board) vigorously contested this case, taking refuge in several technical legal objections, one of which actually questioned the right of the minor to seek the injunction. Justice Kelly expressed dissatisfaction that earlier State commitments and agreed plans given in *FN v. Minister for Education* (1998) were delayed, resulting in the unavailability of appropriate facilities, thus necessitating the detention of non-offending children in penal institutions for accommodation and protection. In an earlier judgment, *DB v. Minister for Justice* (1999), Justice Kelly stated that there was a need for '60 places of either containment or high support to deal with minors of the type involved in this litigation'. Thus he took the unusual step of granting the injunction compelling the Minister for Education to complete two developments. He was also critical firstly of the political response which he believed was neither proportionate, efficient, timeous nor effective and secondly, of the issue of provision of support units which was lost in interdepartmental wranglings over demarcation lines. In the *DB* case, Justice Kelly categorically indicated that the absence of the promised high-support places meant that:

> Young people who are entitled to the benefit of the declaration made by [Justice Geoghegan in *FN* (1995)] will have long since become adults without having had the State discharge the obligations which it owes to them . . . The addressing of the right of the young people that I have dealt with appears to be bogged down in a bureaucratic and administrative quagmire.[40]

One of the most extraordinary and highly questionable aspects of the *ST v. Minister for Health, Education and AG* (2000) case was that the Department argued that the injunction sought lacked specificity and therefore could not be granted. However, Justice Kelly vehemently disagreed, holding that the injunction spelt out no more than what the State has already agreed will be done and merely required the Minister for Health and Children to abide by the evidence already given to the Court – *dictum meum factum*. Even more extraordinary was the contention by the State that all the children represented in the *ST* case had no *locus standi*, i.e. no standing before the Court, and would get no direct benefit from the remedy sought. Justice Kelly also rejected this contention. It was also argued by the State that to grant the children such injunctions was to trespass on the role of the Executive/Cabinet in the determination of child policy. But Justice Kelly stated that he was not making policy since he was merely acting as custodian of children's constitutional rights in which the Government had defaulted and were setting them at nought or trying to circumvent them. All he was doing was merely securing, vindicating and enforcing children's constitutional rights. According to Justice Kelly, not only are children-at-risk disabled socially but:

> they also have a legal disability in that they cannot assert their own constitutional rights: this has to be done on their behalf either by a next friend or a guardian *ad litem*. Normally, a parent would exercise such a right but in many cases involving children like this the parents are either unwilling or unable to do so.[41]

The implications of Justice Kelly's judgment and other similar judgments outlined above are that Irish Courts are compelled to ensure that constitutional rights of troubled minors who require special placements will be vindicated to the point that injunctions sought will be granted – this would ensure that Courts keep faith with their obligations both to such children and the Constitution. The *ST* (2000) judgment has now been appealed by the

State. The decision identifies the precise demarcation and parameters of the Separation of Powers doctrine, which recognises
the separateness of the various organs of the State, i.e. Executive, Legislature and Courts. By injuncting the State to provide
facilities for troubled children it could be argued that the Courts
were trespassing on the jurisdiction of the Executive. Justice
Kelly's reply to this assertion was that he was not offending the
Separation of Powers doctrine because he was simply upholding
constitutional rights of children.

It now seems therefore that if Irish children have any legal
disability within the legal system, such as their inability as
minors to assert their own constitutional rights, then the Irish
judiciary is prepared to take on the role of interventionist champion of children's rights, in the absence of the State's obligation
to protect the most vulnerable and voiceless of minorities in
Irish society.

5. Towards Reform of Children's Rights

*Although most fields of law which involve the application of
legal principles to interpersonal conflict often present
intractable problems, the difficulties presented by attempting to
interpret the law within a framework of children's rights cannot
be underestimated.*

J. Fortin[42]

The proactive role of Irish judges in the context of children's
rights has been a constant feature of Irish jurisprudence prior to
and post the UN Committee's evaluation of Ireland's *Compliance
Report* (1996). Coincidentally, at the time of drafting and submit-
ting the 1996 *Compliance Report to the UN Committee on the Rights
of the Child*, a national fifteen-member expert committee, the
Constitution Review Group, undertook a major re-evaluation of
the Irish Constitution. The Constitution Review Group's restrictive
terms of reference were limited to merely 'review the Constitution, not to rewrite or replace it' and 'to establish those areas
where constitutional change may be desirable or necessary' with

the objective of examining the various constitutional provisions in a 'clear and orderly manner with a résumé of relevant arguments'.[43] One area of constitutional change, which was deemed desirable and necessary by the Group, concerned the status of children's express and implied constitutional rights in Ireland.

The Constitution Review Group published their substantial 701-page report in May 1996, too late for inclusion in the schedule of documents supplied by the Irish Government with their UN *Compliance Report*[44], but sufficiently early for the CRA and other NGOs to incorporate the Constitution Group's relevant recommendations into their respective submissions to the UN Committee. The UN Committee at their deliberation in Geneva in January 1998 was impressed with the general thrust of the Constitution Review Group's recommendations regarding the rights of the child in Ireland.[45] The CRA's submission to the UN Committee, *Small Voices: Vital Rights*, recommended that the Constitution Review Group's recommendations with respect to children 'should be implemented without delay', particularly the recommendation that 'the Constitution be amended to make express provision for the rights of the child'.[46] In its *Concluding Observations Report* (1998) the UN Committee, under the heading 'Positive Aspects' (of which there were only three), referred in general terms to the 'recent efforts undertaken by the State Party [Ireland] in the field of law reform. The Committee welcomes the planned constitutional revision.' Under the heading 'Suggestions and Recommendations' (of which there were eighteen), the UN Committee recommended that:

> The State Party [Ireland] take all appropriate measures to accelerate the implementation of the recommendations of the Constitutional [*sic*] Review Group for the inclusion of all the principles and provisions of the Convention . . . thereby reinforcing the status of the child as a full subject of rights.[47]

One of the radical conclusions of the Constitution Review Group was that Article 41 of the Irish Constitution (The Family) required significant amendments 'some of which raise difficult issues that necessitate the achievement of delicate balances for their resolution'.[48] On the legal status of children within a constitutional framework, the Review Group recommended the express inclusion of the:

> judicially constructed unenumerated rights of children in a coherent manner, particularly those rights which are not guaranteed elsewhere and are peculiar to children.

The Review Group also regarded the UNCRC as an appropriate comparative paradigm for developing children's rights as 'it constitutes a comprehensive compilation of child-specific rights many of which have already been identified by the [Irish] superior courts'. Specifically, the Group examined Articles 3, 7, 9, 18 and 20 of the UNCRC.

The inclusion of children's constitutional rights that were not previously expressly included in the text of the Constitution has some interpretative ramifications for the overall harmonious and delicate balance of the Irish Constitution. Furthermore, privileging children's rights could potentially result in a subsequent diminution of the rights of others, such as parents. A textual and interpretative readjustment of the interrelationship between the rights of adults and children would necessarily follow the insertion of any amendment that might include rights not previously included in the Constitution. The resolution arrived at by the Review Group for such possible legal clashes and conflicts was that:

> If parental rights and children's rights are both being expressly guaranteed, it would be desirable that the Constitution make clear which of these rights should take precedence in the event of a conflict between the rights.

The Constitution Review Group made at least seven specific itemised recommendations on the legal status of children.

Article 7 of the UNCRC was regarded by the Group as having a significant influence on their deliberations and conclusions. Article 7 states: 'That the child shall be registered immediately after birth and shall have the right from birth to a name, the right to acquire a nationality and, as far as possible, the right to know and be cared for by his or her parents.' The Group therefore recommended that a revised Article 41 of the Constitution (The Family) might include:

(a) the right of every child to be registered immediately after birth and to have from birth a name;
(b) the right of every child, as far as practicable, to know his or her parents, subject to the proviso that such right should be subject to regulation by law in the interests of the child.

In the Review Group's view, these two constitutional rights would fill the present legal lacunae for Irish children. By giving children rights to their identity, children would necessarily also be entitled to a knowledge and history of their birth parents. There is no express statutory right under the Adoption Acts 1952-1998 for adoptees to have direct access to information on their natural/biological parent(s). In a recent Supreme Court judgment, *O'T v. B and Rotunda Girls Aid Society* (1998), the issue of the legal rights of adoptees to background information about their biological parents was analysed at length by the Court. Justice Barron stated that:

> The basic question is one of secrecy. This has always been a paramount consideration in adoption law. There has not been any occasion before the courts that that secrecy has been breached . . . It is clearly the policy of the legislature that access to pre-adoption information should be available only in exceptional circumstances.[49]

The Court further declared that a natural mother has a right to privacy which must be balanced against the right of the child to know the identity of the natural parents. The Court also held that neither set of rights is an absolute or unqualified one and its exercise may be restricted by the constitutional rights of others and by the requirement of the common good. Such enabling information on matters like genetic and health background might prove significant for children in the short or long term for physical and/or psychological reasons.

Other recommendations of the Review Group included the right of every child, as far as practicable, to be cared for by his or her parents, i.e. *both* parents. This recommendation was advanced in order to give some substance to the present precarious and uncertain legal relationship between a putative unmarried biological father and his child where the child is a non-marital child. Under traditional Irish common law principles a child born out of wedlock was classified legally as illegitimate or as a *filius nullius* – a son of no man with no recognised legal relations with their parents and no inheritance rights. Legally this situation has now changed to the extent of giving biological fathers some rights in relation to their child.

In 1998, the UN Committee also expressed similar concerns about Irish children's rights to have contact with *both* their parents, especially in a non-marital context whereby a biological father's name was not always entered on a child's birth certificate. The UN Committee's *Concluding Observations* (1998) specifically highlighted the 'disadvantaged situation of [Irish] children, born from unmarried parents, due to the lack of appropriate procedures to include the identity of the father in the birth registration of the child'. The UN Committee recommended that Ireland take 'appropriate measures for establishing, as far as possible, procedures for the inclusion of the name of the father in the birth certificate of children born from unmarried parents'[50] in order to be consistent with the tenets and principles of the UNCRC. In general, there is much criticism of the continued near absolute constitutional exclusion of unmarried fathers in Ireland. This ostracisation has impacted adversely on those fathers who have established a relationship with their child. Few supporting positive arguments have been advanced judicially or through statute law for giving automatic constitutional rights to every unmarried/biological father merely by virtue of mere biological links which might include paternity resulting from rape, incest or sperm donorship.

In Ireland, the introduction of the Status of Children Act 1987 went some way towards accommodating the rights of children in relation to accessibility to both parents where and when appropriate. This legislation gave an unmarried father a mere statutory right *to apply* to the courts for appointment as joint guardian and/or custodian or gaining access rights regarding his child. Such an application is fraught with uncertainties. The salient provision of the Act stipulates that:

> Where the father and mother of an infant have not married each other, the Court may on application of the father by order appoint him to be guardian of the infant.

By contrast, the unmarried mother in Ireland is constitutionally (under Article 40.3) and statutorily the automatic presumed sole guardian and custodian of her child. If the natural mother supported the natural father's application for guardianship, success would be almost assured. The primary objective of the 1987 Act was the equalisation of statutory rights between children born outside marriage with those born within marriage. Parental rights (if any) under this legislation are subject to the Court regarding the welfare of the child as the first and paramount consideration as provided in section 3 of the Guardianship of Infants Act 1964 which states that:

> Where in any proceedings before any court, the custody, guardianship or upbringing of an infant is in question, the Court in deciding that question, shall regard the welfare of the infant as the first and paramount consideration.

Non-marital Irish children are now statutorily entitled to succeed to their father's estate, to be supported and maintained by both parents and to be legitimated by the subsequent marriage of their parents. Also there is no provision in the 1987 Act compelling the biological father to be appointed automatically guardian of the non-marital child. Similarly, no provision exists facilitating a child's application to the Court to have its father appointed as guardian. In *JK v. VW* (1990), the Irish Supreme Court elaborated on the statutory powers conferred on courts to appoint a natural father as guardian of a child. Chief Justice Finlay stated that:

> The blood-link between the infant and the father and the possibility for the infant to have the benefit of the guardianship by and the society of its father is one of the many factors which may be viewed by the Court as relevant to its welfare.

In the same case, Justice McCarthy's conclusion on the matter was that he found 'it difficult to accept that a loving father, who with the mother, wanted to have a child, has no natural right to the society of the child'.[51] In *WO'R v. EH (Guardianship)* (1996), Justice Murphy stated that: 'Fatherhood in conjunction with a long-standing and acting commitment to the welfare of the child is a factor to which the trial judge is bound to give serious consideration and . . . may well be of decisive importance'. Chief Justice Hamilton in his judgment in *WO'R* stated that: 'There may be considerations appropriate to the welfare of the child that make it desirable for the child to enjoy the society, protection and guardianship of his or her father'. Viewed globally, however, the jurisprudence in these various cases confirms the natural father's legally inferior position under Irish law and unmarried fathers also continue to be denied the same constitutional recognition as that offered to unmarried mothers. The net effect of the *WO'R* case is that it seems that judicial emphasis is now being placed not so much on a father's rights to the society of his child but rather on the rights of a child to the society of its father.

Alan Shatter is critical of this legal impoverishment of natural fathers *vis-à-vis* their legal relationship with their child. He suggests that:

> It is arguable that the current legal regime fails to properly recognise and reflect the family ties between unmarried fathers and their children and is 'mother-centred' rather than 'child-centred'. The primary focus should be the best interests of the child. It is accepted as a matter of public policy that it is in the interests of a child's welfare and development to foster a close relationship between a child born within marriage and both of the child's parents. Consequently, there is no basis for a different approach being applied to children born outside marriage except in certain exceptional circumstances.[52]

With effect from 1 October 1997 the statutory birth registration procedures for the natural father of a non-marital child were updated by the Registration of Births Act 1996.[53] This legislation provides for the inclusion of the name of the natural father with the assent of the natural mother. The father's name may be registered only in the following consensual circumstances:

(a) both parents must attend the Registrar's Office personally to sign the Register; or

(b) the mother must provide a declaration made by her giving the identity of the father. The mother's declaration must be accompanied by the father's statutory declaration expressly acknowledging paternity; or

(c) the mother or father must produce a certified copy of a Court order naming the father of the child in proceedings relating to guardianship or maintenance of a child.

The new requirements regarding the extensive information to be included in a birth certificate go some way towards upholding a child's right to have an authentic and full identity as well as a right to know both parents.

If the 1996 Constitution Review Group's clarion call for reform of Irish child law coincided with the deliberations and conclusions of the UN Committee's dissection of Ireland's 1996 *Compliance Report*, significant legislative changes were also introduced at around the same time heralding a trend towards developing a series of domestic statutory laws which had indirect and direct positive implications for children's rights in the Republic of Ireland. The child law reforms, advocated by the Constitution Review Group, were given partial expression in the general child-centred philosophy of the Children Act 1997, which updated the law on guardianship, custody of and access to children.[54]

Similarly, the Adoption Act 1998, which gave a minor yet effective consultative role to some unmarried fathers in the domestic adoption process, increased the possibilities and expectations of greater interpersonal involvement between the non-marital child and its biological father. The Adoption Act 1998 broadly adheres to the Review Group's recommendations that (a) every child has the right, as far as practicable, to be cared for by his or her parents; and (b) every child has the right to be reared with due regard to his or her welfare. Perhaps more importantly from an international child law perspective, recent Irish legislation seems now to adhere to the general spirit of Article 9 (3) of the UNCRC which stipulates that the child who is separated from one or both parents has a right 'to maintain personal relations and direct contact with both parents on a regular basis, except if it is contrary to the child's best interests'. Article 18 (1) of the UNCRC gives additional substantive legal possibilities to the unmarried father. It states that:

> State Parties shall use their best efforts to ensure recognition of the principle that both parents have common responsibilities for the upbringing and development of the child. Parents or, as the case may be, legal guardians, have the primary responsibility for the upbringing and development of the child. The best interests of the child will be their basic concern.[55]

In England and Wales the statutory legal status of the unmarried father is regulated by the Children Act 1989. The English judiciary has been at pains in recent years to facilitate the evolution of some parental rights to the unmarried father for the sake of the child's welfare and interests. *Re H (Minors) (Local Authority: Parental Rights)* (1991),[56] Lord Justice Balcombe set down three principal factors which were to assist the courts in granting family rights to the unmarried father:

(a) the degree of commitment which the father has shown towards the child;

(b) the degree of attachment which exists between the father and the child; or

(c) the reasons of the father applying for the order.[57]

It seems therefore that UK judges are anxious that 'wherever possible, the law should confer on a concerned father that stamp of approval because he has shown himself willing and anxious to pick up the responsibility of fatherhood and not to deny or avoid it.' This is not always the situation in Ireland and therefore many children are deprived of a potential relationship that, in all likelihood, would be for the betterment of the child.

6. The Children Act 1997 – New Millennium Potential

The Irish child care system is unique in that it has resisted the steady erosion of parental rights that has characterised the international child care system . . . While the menu of issues and unresolved problems can seem overwhelming, there has nonetheless been a notable movement towards child-centred legislation in Ireland. The realisation of a vibrant and flourishing child-centred statutory system will mean that we have to discard the shackles of our adult-centred past.

G. Shannon [58]

Conor Power has described the Children Act 1997 as the most innovative contemporary child-centred legislation containing 'some of the most important changes in parent and child law ever introduced into Ireland'.[59] The UN Committee in January

1998 had called for the immediate 'implementation of the Children Act 1997, thereby reinforcing the status of the child as a full subject of rights'. While the Children Act 1997 was making its way through the Oireachtas the *Final Report of the Commission on the Family: 'Strengthening Families for Life'* (1998) was also published.[60]

The Commission on the Family was established in October 1995 to examine the effects of legislation and policies on families and make recommendations to the Government on proposals, which would strengthen the capacity of families to carry out their functions in a changing economic and social environment. This Family Commission undertook empirical research *inter alia* on fathers and their domestic role in family life and an overview of family policy in Ireland. The Report contained a comprehensive and in-depth analysis of the issues affecting Irish families as well as wide-ranging recommendations across several different policy areas. One of the central suggestions made by the Commission on the Family in relation to children was that:

> Family policy must have regard to the principle that continuity and stability are major requirements in family relationships. Continuity and stability should be recognised as having a major value for individual well-being and social stability especially as far as children are concerned. Joint parenting should be encouraged with a view to ensuring that, as far as possible, children have the opportunity of developing close relationships with both parents. In cases where joint parenting is in the child's best interest, public policy has a key role in promoting that interest.[61]

Indeed the Family Commission had a particular concern to prioritise the needs of children on the basis that public policy ought to be particularly concerned with protecting the vulnerable members in families. The Commission thus pointed to the role of public policy as a means of promoting and enhancing the position of children in families and in their community and promoting their well-being. The 1996 Census data had indicated that in total there were 31,298 family units consisting of cohabiting couples in 1996. Of this 18,640 (60%) were couples without children. Of the remaining 12,658 family units, 52% had one child while a further 28% had two children. Overall, cohabiting couples accounted for 3% of all Irish families in 1996 in the Republic of Ireland. The Commission was particularly concerned, given the findings in the 1996 National Census, about the changing and varied family units in Irish society in which children were living their daily lives.

The enactment of the Children Act 1997 in Ireland was generally regarded as a 'welcome step forward in the on-going process of the promotion of children's rights'. On the negative side, however, the 1997 Act was considered to represent a 'missed opportunity to review the whole area of children's rights and to either consolidate or overhaul existing legislation'. The 1997 Act was further criticised for failing to go far enough in reviewing the basic concepts involved in modern family relationships. The 1997 Act is certainly not a codifying or consolidating Act nor does it attempt to ameliorate the fragmented nature of Irish child law.

If the UN Committee in their 1998 Report had characterised Ireland's approach to children's rights as 'fragmented' and 'devoid of a national strategy', a reading of the long title to the Children Act 1997 would readily confirm those deep reservations of the UN Committee. There is no major statutory provision for structural and functional co-ordination between the various Ministries which attempt to deal effectively and systematically with children. However, in 1999 a statutory instrument was introduced which delegated and allocated significant responsibilities to a Minister of State on child-related matters.[62] This is as close as the Irish Government has come to establishing a Minister for Children. The existing institutional overlapping on child law matters has not been remedied by the introduction of the Children Act 1997 which also continues to view the child within a family context rather than as an autonomous individual as recommended by the UN Committee. However, according to the UN Committee, the 1997 Act seemed to introduce some necessary reform which might 'not adequately reflect a children's rights base approach' – the legislation does respond to children's advocates who argued for some change regarding the regulations governing guardianship, custody and access of marital and non-marital children, with an ancillary consequence of lessening the legal discrimination, indifference and hostility towards biological fathers even if they aspired to or actually performed a 'caring role' *vis-à-vis* their child.

The Children Act 1997 introduced a major change of terminology which at one level seems trite, yet exemplifies a modern evolving view of children. The term 'infant' and its related forms are removed from the principal child-related legislation (Guardianship of Infants Act 1964 and section 9 of the Status of Children Act 1987) and replaced with the terms 'child' and 'children'.[63] Altering key concepts in the public and private aspects of family and child law can have significant positive consequences for procedural and substantive legal issues. The Children Act 1989 (England and Wales), for example, introduced some fundamental changes of concept which altered the legal landscape relating to the care and upbringing of children. This latter legislation was responsible for 'parenthood' replacing guardianship as the primary concept, and 'parental responsibility' replacing the concept of parental rights and duties.[64] According to Justice Hale, a senior British judge, the objective of introducing such a vital new concept of 'parental responsibility' was 'to emphasise the practical reality that bringing up children is a serious responsibility, rather than a matter of legal rights'.[65]

The essential multi-purpose thrust of the Children Act 1997 was to amend and significantly improve the law in relation to guardianship, custody, access and maintenance of children. In addition, Section 21 of the Children Act 1997 permits expressly the use of video-link evidence for the first time in civil proceedings concerning a child's welfare. The Irish Courts can now hear the evidence, either on oath or not, from a child through live television link which may be given within the State or outside the State. The questioning of a child may be done through an intermediary. This new private law provision marks a significant departure from the standard procedure of giving evidence. It also represents a shift of procedural emphasis by acknowledging the obvious vulnerability of children in such proceedings, accommodating them in the most vital of court tasks – that of giving evidence in an adult context. Hearsay evidence of children is also now admissible and can be heard in legal proceedings.[66] Justice O'Flaherty has stated in the Supreme Court, in *Southern Health Board v. CH* (1996), that:

> it is well to point out that a courtroom is, in general, an
> unsuitable environment for a child of tender years.

The Children Act 1997 also confers a degree of equality between non-marital parents in relation to their legal relationship with their child on the basis of a consensual agreement without the need to resort to formal court proceedings. Non-marital parents of a child can now agree to declare by means of a statutory declaration, subject to fulfilling certain conditions, that they are the parents of the child. With this new simplified procedure the biological/natural mother can agree to appoint the natural father as a joint guardian of the child.[67] The sworn declaratory parenthood procedure requires the mother and father to declare that they are the mother and father of the child, that the mother agrees to the appointment of the father as guardian of the child and that arrangements are in place regarding custody.

There is also an option to agree access. These provisions in the legislation represent a successful attempt to adopt an indirect child-orientated approach towards securing the rights of children to the society of their non-marital parents. Ward suggests that the novel use of 'agreement' terminology as opposed to 'consenting' language in the statutory declaration form represents a movement away from the unilateralism of a mother's 'consent' to the appointment. For Ward 'the concept of each parent agreeing gives the impression of equality between parents'.[68] An unfortunate lacuna in the Act however is the absence of procedures for dispensing with the mother's agreement should she withhold her consent unreasonably and should there be compelling reasons affecting the child's best interest for dispensing with the mother's consent.

In common with other common law jurisdictions, Ireland has had to give serious consideration in private law proceedings to the question of access to and custody of children by third parties and more remote relatives, such as to include those related by blood or marriage. The rights of the child in relation to its extended family through the bloodline or through marriage is beginning to gain currency and acceptance inside and outside Irish courts. It is readily acknowledged that new forms of family units have emerged and become acceptable. It is in this context that non-parental access rights to children has become one of the novel, yet salient, issues adequately addressed in the Children Act 1997. Prior to this Act, the Irish High Court in *MD v. GD* (1993) indicated that access orders were primarily for the welfare of the child and were thus a basic right of the *child* as opposed to a parental right. Justice Mella Carroll indicated that access orders allowed:

> . . . the child access to persons other than its natural parents. It is the welfare of the child that is paramount. For example, if there were a child in the custody of its mother who lived with her parents, and the father had limited access, then the mother died; if the father claims and gets custody, it seems to me that access by the maternal grandparents, if contested could be granted on the basis that it would be for the benefit of the child to maintain links with its grandparents . . . it is the right of the child with which the court is concerned, not the right of the adult.[69]

This judgment together with the Children Act 1997 are in keeping with a cluster of judgments from the European Court of Human Rights since 1983 which have asserted that the reciprocal mutual enjoyment by a child and parent of each other's company may constitute a fundamental dimension of family life whereby the access right of a child is near automatic subject to only limited exceptions. An example is *Eriksson v. Sweden* (1989), in which the European Court of Human Rights held that curtailment or denial of a child's access right violated Article 8. Article 9 (3) of the UNCRC, which is similar to this 'Eriksson principle', provides for: 'the right of the child who is separated from one or both parents to maintain personal relations and direct contact with both parents on a regular basis, except if it is contrary to the child's best interests'.

The Children Act 1997 grants quite radical powers to courts to consider applications for access from relatives of a child as well as applications from those who have acted *in loco parentis* to a child. One focus of this legislation is to respect and secure those wider relationships in order to secure the best interests of the child. The term 'relative' is not expressly defined in the Act but probably includes grandparents, adult aunts and uncles.[70] When deciding whether a relative can proceed with an access application a court shall have regard to all the circumstances, including in particular;

  (a) the applicant's connection with the child;
  (b) the risk, if any, of the application disrupting the child's life to the extent that the child would be harmed by it and;
  (c) the wishes of the child's guardian.

This conditional right by a relative to apply is a two-stage procedure whereby the permission of the court is a necessary prerequisite before applying for an actual access order. The preliminary first stage/procedural legal hurdle is presumably to exclude vexatious, trivial and unmeritorious applications as well as operating as a means of protecting children. It is the 'welfare' test which determines the substantive application for access.[71]

This piecemeal development of child access law is perhaps a minor triumph for children's rights in Ireland resulting in a more expansive view of a child's legal position within the extended family. However, the spectre of Article 41 of the Irish Constitution continues, in an omnipresent manner, to hover over all legislation that attempts to restrict the principle of parental autonomy. One of the inherent shortcomings in the Act is the failure to provide for indirect access as an interim measure for appropriate circumstances where applicants may still be regarded as persons who could contribute to the child's welfare to the extent that the child would benefit from maintaining that indirect access arrangement.

By contrast, under public law child care proceedings, the Child Care Act 1991 obliges Health Boards to facilitate reasonable access to a child by a parent, a person acting *in loco parentis* or any other person who, in the opinion of the board, has a *bona fide* interest in the child, and such access may include allowing the child to reside temporarily with such persons. Although there is no express provision entitling a child to apply for access it would seem that a child's Guardian *ad litem* (see next section) could supply that role as a person with an unequivocal *bona fide* interest in the child.[72]

7. Children's Representation in Legal Proceedings

Consulting with children means more than asking them what they think. It means ensuring that they have adequate information appropriate to their age with which to form opinions. It means being provided with meaningful opportunities to express their views and explore options open to them and it means having those views listened to, respected and considered seriously.

G. Landsdown.[73]

The recognition of Irish children as juristic rights-bearing persons with particular rights in some private family and child law matters has been given further substance in section 11 of the Children Act 1997. This authorises the appointment of a Guardian *ad litem* (GAL) in such private law proceedings as guardianship, custody and access where the child is not a party to the proceedings.[74] This provision, however, is not mandatory. Until 1991 no statutory provision existed empowering Courts to appoint a GAL in Family Law proceedings involving children. The Parliamentary *Dáil* and *Seanad Debates* on the Child Care Act 1991 provide some definitional indicators of the role of the guardian *ad litem*:

> Their role is to represent the child, take care of the child, observe the child and ensure that the child's interests are protected beyond any doubt in the care proceedings. (*Dail Debates*, 1991).
>
> The role of the guardian *ad litem* will be to interview the child, to assess his or her needs, to inform the court of those needs and of the child's wishes. (*Dail Debates*, 1991)
>
> Guardians *ad litem* are court-appointed professionals who have a very specific and independent role in relation to children who are the subject of court hearings. The main job of the guardian *ad litem* is to focus very specifically on the interests of the child and report to the court for the purposes of the court hearings. It is not intended that the relationship is an ongoing or therapeutic one. It is contemplated solely with regard to the court and comes into play where the parent is absent through illness, death or incompetence of various kinds or is a party to contentious proceedings. (*Seanad Debates*, 1991)

In child law matters the Court, which has the ultimate discretion and capacity in the appointment process, is obliged to consider various criteria when deciding whether or not to appoint this 'child's voice phenomenon'. In Irish public law proceedings involving children the Child Care Act 1991 stipulates the appointment process regarding a GAL, particularly in child care proceedings where children are ill-treated, neglected or abused. A recent highly publicised example of the operation of the GAL system in a child sexual abuse context was the *C case*. 'C' was a minor who was raped, and the issue before the Courts was the possible termination of the pregnancy. A GAL was appointed by the Court in order to represent the child in the proceedings.[75]

The extension and elaboration into private law proceedings of the GAL child-centred statutory system of giving children a voice in judicial and administrative proceedings affecting children[76] is possible only if there are 'special circumstances of the case [and] it is necessary in the best interests of the child to do so'. Appointment of a Guardian *ad litem* may also be ordered on the basis of the Court having regard to five particular criteria:

a) the age and understanding of the child;

b) any report on any question affecting the welfare of the child that is furnished to the court under section 47 of the Family Law Act 1995,

c) the welfare of the child;

d) whether and to what extent the child should be given the opportunity to express its wishes in the proceedings, taking into account any statement in relation to those matters in any report under section 47 of the Family Law Act 1995; and

e) any submission made in relation to the matter of the appointment as a Guardian *ad litem* that is made to the Court by or on behalf of a party to the proceedings or any other person to whom they relate.

The 1997 legislation gives no indication as to the precise legal weight to be given to each of those factors or whether the Court is to view them globally as an interrelated inextricable package of items. Recent academic research indicates that the list serves a dual function:

> Firstly, it aids and directs the court during its decision-making. Secondly, as a guide, it contributes to the accountability of the Court's decision-making.[77]

The judicial decision authorising the appointment of a GAL is merely discretionary and not mandatory. On this and other related matters (guardianship, custody and access) the Children Act 1997 expressly addresses the approach which Irish Courts must now adopt towards ascertaining the child's wishes. It is now mandatory for Courts, where appropriate and practicable, to take into account the wishes of the child 'having regard to the age and understanding of the child'. The precise nature and scope of the phrase 'having regard to' is as yet undefined with no judicial gloss so far ascribed to it. When contrasted with the noticeably paternalistic approach of previous children's legislation, this Act facilitates a child's right to be present at part or all of the hearing of the proceedings if the child so requests. This right, however, is significantly modified by a subsequent proviso that Courts shall only accede to such requests if it appears to the Court 'having regard to the age of the child or the nature of the proceedings, it would not be in the child's best interests'. Regrettably, unlike the Child Care Act 1991 for public law child issues, the 1997 Act does not expressly permit children to have their own legal representation nor are they entitled to be joined as parties to proceedings in family law disputes. In the absence of express statutory authority for granting separate legal representation to children[78] it has been suggested that perhaps the Courts have an inherent jurisdiction for the appointment of a solicitor for a child, who is made a party to private law proceedings.

The *Denham Commission Report* (1999) expressed significant reservations about the potential for accentuating unnecessarily the adversarial nature of private family law proceedings with the provision for the separate representation of children in particular cases. The Report's conclusion on the point was that such a legal option could:

> create as many problems – costs, delay, an increase in the adversarial nature of the proceedings – as it solves. In many cases separate representation of the child is not really necessary as the welfare of the child can be ascertained through expert or other evidence.[79]

Indeed the gradual process of conferring statutory rights on children to direct or indirect representation in Irish legal proceedings has been a slow yet evolving one, but the current trend is towards increasing that representation. According to Bainham:

> The essential feature of child representation in the modern law is that in *public* law cases it will be the rule rather than the exception while in *private* law cases it will be the exception rather than the rule. The effect of this divergent policy is to preserve, at least on this issue, a distinct dichotomy of public and private children cases.[80]

This academic comment could aptly apply to child law in Ireland. The GAL sections of the 1997 legislation have been criticised as being 'short on detail'. There is also a potential conflict of interests in section 28 (3) which envisages, where appropriate, the appointment of the expert witness/social worker (from whom a report on a child was procured) as a GAL.[81] The *Sixth Report of the Working Group on a Courts Commission* (1999), which was established to evaluate critically the structures and functions of the Irish Courts' system, concurred with the recommendation of the earlier *Law Reform Commission Report on Family Courts* (1996). The latter Report stated that social workers who devise reports for Courts on children's welfare were a category of professionals deemed suitable for appointment as GALs.[82] This fusion of roles for social workers poses potential ethical and legal difficulties. There are significant differences between the role of a social worker as an expert witness and their role as a GAL.

In March 1999 the British Lord Chancellor's Department addressed this dilemma in a research paper. English/Welsh jurisprudence on GALs is considerable, especially on such matters as their duties, selection and the setting up of local authority panels of potential guardians. English legislation also provides for the establishment of complaints boards and for panel managers – for training and for standards.[83] No comparable provisions are included in Irish child law statutes nor do there appear to be specific powers in the Children Act 1997 to make regulations which might provide for such necessarily detailed matters to be dealt with by way of statutory instruments. Alan Shatter has alluded to the paucity of statutory detail regulating the GAL position generally in public law proceedings. He notes that:

> The Act [Child Care Act 1991] gives the Court no guidance as to who should be regarded as qualified to act as guardian *ad litem* nor does it contain any provision to ensure a person so acting is entirely independent of both the Health Board that brought the proceedings and the child's parents or other custodians. Even more curiously, the Act fails to prescribe the duties of a person so appointed.[84]

Similar criticisms apply almost as much to Section 28 of the Children Act 1997, which has remarkably little detail as to the qualification, and independence of a GAL. The *Report on Irish Family Courts* (1996) had strongly recommended the extension of the service into private law proceedings:

> . . . the court should have the power, in any proceedings which affect a child (i.e. not just care proceedings), to appoint a guardian *ad litem* where the court is satisfied that it is in the interests of the child and in the interests of justice to do so. The guardian *ad litem* is not a substitute for a legal representative, but should be an option where the court considers that something more than the standard social report is required for its adjudication. An independent panel of social workers should be established from which the court may appoint guardians *ad litem*.[85]

In the recent *Code of Practice Report* (1995) of the Incorporated Law Society of Ireland, it is now recommended to those solicitors who are engaged in cases involving children that:

> The Solicitor must keep in mind that the interests of the children do not necessarily coincide with the interests

of either parent. In certain cases, separate representation may be necessary in order to preserve the independent rights of the child. It is a matter which might be considered by the solicitor and, if necessary, brought to the attention of the Court.

The *Denham Commission Report* (1999) advocated that 'the policy on [legal representation of children] as contained in the 1997 Act should be reviewed in the light of experience of its operation, particularly with a view to giving to the Court power to appoint guardians *ad litem*.

A final criticism of the 1997 Act is the manifest omission of a provision for the appointment of an independent legal representative to act on behalf of a child as an alternative or in addition to the Guardian *ad litem*. The Child Care Act 1991 expressly provides for the appointment of independent legal representation in public law proceedings. The *LRC Report on Family Courts* (1996) recommended that such a measure be included in children's private law proceedings. Perhaps the drafters of the 1997 Act regarded such a legal support system as wholly necessary only for public child care proceedings which require a higher level of state intervention, and not so immediate or essential for perceived less grave circumstances in private law proceedings. This latter point concurs with Bainham's view that 'child representation in *private* law cases will be the exception rather than the rule'.[86]

The argument outlined earlier, concerning the avoidance of accentuating the adversarial nature of family law proceedings, is quite persuasive. More convincing, however, is the resource implications argument which highlights the State's incapacity, even in child-related matters, to provide every resource necessary to protect or assert a child's legal right. On this latter point Professor Freeman has noted that: 'Minimalism and residualism in the State's approach to children's welfare at a policy level are still evident in the lack of a right to appropriate representation for children.'[87] He also argues that there are significant dangers inherent in child-related legislation which falls short of taking children's rights seriously. He suggests that '[children's] rights without services are meaningless, and services without resources cannot be provided'. Finally he concludes that:

> The importance of legislation as a symbol cannot be underestimated, but the true recognition of children's rights requires implementation in practice. Indeed, unimplemented, partially implemented or badly implemented laws, may actually do children more harm than good.

Creating an improved legal framework such as the Children Act 1997 or indeed any other child legislation will founder if resourced inadequately. Freeman's terse judgment on under-resourcing by Governments in this area of child law is that:

> . . . children are not interested in symbolic politics. Ultimately, the question of rights for children resolves into questions of distributive justice. If we are not prepared to accept this, we may as well give up the fight to see children's rights improved.[88]

The Irish Supreme Court in *Southern Health Board v. CH* (1996) has recently undertaken a gradual redressing of the legal balance in favour of children by stating that: 'The Guardianship of Infants Act 1964 . . . reinforces the common law position that the Court is entrusted with the responsibility of the child's welfare'. This judgment probably represents an organic alteration in the procedural and substantive ethos of children's cases as determined by the Courts. This case also created an exception to the hearsay evidence rule stating that Courts have discretion in admitting such evidence. This particular case involved the admissibility of a child's video evidence. Statutory expression is now given to this exception in section 23 of the Children Act 1997.

It is universally acknowledged that legal proceedings can be an anguishing and harrowing experience for children. Automatic provision of a GAL and/or independent legal representation for children in public and private law proceedings should be the presumptive norm in Irish law. This would be the clearest sign by politicians and policy makers of their authentic resolve to protect children's rights. If properly resourced, structured and regulated, the GAL strengthens the child's availability to appropriate legal representation, ensuring that they are given the capability of being heard either directly or through a representative in any judicial or administrative proceeding.

The current situation in Ireland with the absence of clear rules or guidelines on the ambit of the GAL's powers and duties is unacceptable. Similarly, present legislation does not expressly indicate the need for the GAL to be an 'independent and disinterested party' in the proceedings ensuring that the child's interests and welfare are fully explored and reported to the Court. Recent statutory innovations (outlined above) have nevertheless contributed in a minimal yet positive way to a proper consideration of children's interests and welfare in judicial and/or administrative proceedings. Making those legal proceedings less adversarial lessens any detrimental effects on children.[89] Justice Catherine McGuinness has recently indicated at a conference on the theme of 'Separate Representation of Children' that in her view the Irish judiciary does not favour children being present in Court while cases concerning them are being heard. Viewed optimistically, the Irish GAL system represents a milestone in child representation notwithstanding the serious deficit of regulatory detail as to the GAL's precise powers and duties.

8. Has Irish Child Law Come of Age?

Children's rights are being taken more seriously than was the case a generation ago.

M. Freeman.[90]

The current extensive proposals of the Law Reform Commission (1996) for the establishment of fifteen Irish regional Family Courts give grounds for optimism that family law matters in general and child law in particular will be treated as serious distinct legal matters/areas of law. No longer can Irish family/child law be regarded as an 'uninteresting supplement to property law'.[91] However, there is always an inherent danger peculiar to family law proceedings involving reform of the Courts' structures and functions, and it is the risk of a growing tendency towards excessive informality bordering on the potential delegalisation of family/child law.[92]

Recent developments in child-related legislation, with a marked focus on its child-centred nature, represent a significant shift from the traditional adult-centred nature of the law and a gradual abandonment of the restrictive shackles which were the hallmark of orthodox Irish family law. Judicial interpretations of the statutory landscape have resulted in a sophisticated body of jurisprudence of a somewhat paternalistic nature. But more significantly, Irish judges have now been to the fore in proactively establishing the nature and scope of children's substantive legal rights as well as their procedural rights. Justice Mella Carroll in the High Court has expanded our understanding of the precise nature of procedural rights of children in Irish Courts. She stated that: 'In matters relating to children it is never advisable to lay down stringent practice rules. The matter should always remain flexible'.[93] In the case of *MD v. GD* (1993), which involved the custody and access arrangements regarding a child, she began the newly evolving notion in Irish child law that access arrangements or parental contact arrangements are essentially child-centred. Thus Justice Carroll altered the adult-centred emphasis in access disputes in family courts. Later in the same judgment she stated that:

> A judge is entitled to make an access order to allow the
> child access to persons other than natural parents. It is
> the welfare of the child which is paramount. It is the
> right of the child with which the court is concerned, not
> the right of the adult.

In May 1999 some of the Rules of Court for regulating and
resolving disputes regarding custody guardianship and upbringing of children were radically revised in order to meet the
challenges of the twenty-first century.[94] The Irish Supreme Court
has also lately acknowledged the inappropriateness of strict
adversarial procedures for child care proceedings. Justice O'Flaherty, on behalf of the Supreme Court, enunciated the principle
that there exists a judicial constitutional obligation which
prioritises and 'mandates as a prime consideration, the interests
of the child in any legal proceedings . . . the courtroom is, in
general, an unsuitable environment for a child of tender
years.'[95] In *MF v. Superintendent of Ballymun Garda Station*
(1991)[96] Justice O'Flaherty indicated that generally in child care
proceedings children should not be in Court unless the Court
specifically directs the necessity of their presence. He further
noted that:

> Cases concerning the care and custody of children and
> the protection of their rights are in a special and, possi-
> bly, unique category. Certainly they are special because
> they concern children and are possibly unique in that
> fundamental rights of persons are at issue in litigation
> in which they are not represented . . . a court's *prima
> facie* not a suitable environment for such children.[97]

Chief Justice Finlay, in the same case, noted the urgent need
for 'more efficient and simpler procedure for the protection of
children available to the Courts.'[98] The Irish Supreme Court has
also noted the uniqueness of child care proceedings which it

regards as essentially an inquiry into what is the best for the child in the particular circumstances.

In *The Southern Health Board v. CH* (1996) the issue to be determined was a custody dispute between the 'father of the child' and the Health Board. Aged six, the child was placed voluntarily by the father in the Health Board's care following the death of the child's mother. In custody proceedings under the Guardianship of Infants Act 1964, Justice O'Flaherty stated that:

> The 1964 Act, itself a statutory statement of what is inherent in the Constitution, reinforces the common law position that the court is entrusted with the responsibility of the child's welfare. This is of the utmost importance . . . Here the court must undertake an investigation of what is in the best interests of the child . . . the judge is in essence required to inquire as to what is in the best interests of the child . . . the rights of the father must [also] be safeguarded, as far as practicable . . . But when the consequences of any encroachment on the respective rights is concerned, it is easy to comprehend that the child's welfare must always be of far graver concern to the court. We must, as judges, always harken to the constitutional command which mandates, as a prime consideration, the interests of the child in any legal proceedings.[99]

Commenting on this progressive judicial principle, Shatter has noted that:

> . . . this judgment marks the first tentative steps by the Irish Supreme Court within the existing constitutional framework to elevate children's rights to a higher constitutional plane by the procedural device of applying an inquisitorial rather than an adversarial approach to the resolution of disputes concerning the custody, care and upbringing of children. It remains to be seen whether the judgment of the Supreme Court in *Southern Health Board v. CH* has created the space to allow the court to further develop the law in order to give a priority and

paramountcy to the welfare of the child in all custody
disputes . . . [100]

Within the public law context of children's rights, and in
particular child abuse circumstances, there have been further
significant statutory developments since 1998 which, when
viewed globally and collectively, make considerable advances
towards expressly protecting children who have been abused
and neglected. The Protection for Persons Reporting Child Abuse
Act 1998 provides additional protection for children in Irish
society. The objective of this Act is simply to remove existing
evidential obstacles to the reporting of child abuse or neglect.
The Act creates statutory protective immunity from civil liability
for those who make *bone fide* reports of abuse. The communication of the report can be in writing or otherwise, to the police or
other designated officers of a Health Board. Section 6 of the Act
states expressly that this statutory immunity is in addition to,
and not in substitution for, the pre-existing common law privi-
leges and defences.[101] As in other jurisdictions, fear of being
sued for defamation tends to act as a deterrent to the reporting
of child abuse. In the *Consultation Paper of the Law Reform
Commission on Child Sexual Abuse* (1989) the Commission stated
that legislation should be enacted 'expressly conferring immunity from liability for *bona fide* reports [of child abuse] made with
due care'.[102] The subsequent *Report of the LRC on Child Sexual
Abuse* (1990)[103] repeated its earlier recommendation stating that:

> We would emphasise that the need for the statutory
> immunity [from liability] arises whether or not manda-
> tory report laws are introduced. At present, fear of legal
> proceedings, though frequently misplaced, is operating
> as a serious disincentive to the reporting of suspected
> sexual abuse.

On 21 January 1999, two days before the Act was to come
into effect, the Minister for Health and Children issued a Directive to each Health Board appointing seventeen categories of

Health Board officers as designated persons under the legislation. The categories are:

- Social workers
- public health nurses
- psychiatrists
- child care workers
- hospital consultants
- non-consultant hospital doctors
- all other Health Board medical and dental personnel
- community welfare officers
- all Health Board nursing personnel
- psychologists
- physiotherapists
- health education officers
- and finally, care assistants.
- speech and language therapists
- radiographers
- occupational therapists
- substance abuse counsellors

These categories were appointed as designated officers on the basis that they were the most appropriate official authorities capable of fully investigating such abuse complaints. By providing a general immunity from civil liability for damages and/or any other form of relief to those who act reasonably and in good faith in reporting child abuse (where there are reasonable grounds for believing that abuse has occurred)[104], the Oireachtas has avoided, *pro tem*, the policy and logistical issues which would have to be addressed if mandatory reporting legislation on child abuse were introduced. The *bona fide* reporter must have reasonable grounds for believing that a child is a victim of abuse to the extent that the child has been or is being assaulted, ill-treated, neglected or sexually abused, or that a child's health, development or welfare has been or is being avoidably impaired or neglected.[105] One of the unintended yet legally significant features of this legislation is the alteration of the definition of the concept of the 'welfare' of a child. Welfare was previously confined to the religious, moral, intellectual, physical, and social welfare of the child. This is the first statutory reference to welfare which expressly includes 'emotional' as a factor.[106] In a recent High Court judgment, *DFO'S v. CA* (1999), Justice Catherine McGuinness stated that 'the judges were now adding the word "emotional" to the statutory definition for welfare of the child'. There is no immunity for a *bona fide* report where a child's health, development or welfare *is likely to be* avoidably impaired or neglected. It seems that the parliamentary drafters regarded the latter type of reportage as being too subjective, and accordingly confined the reporting requirement to actual abuse circumstances as distinct from potential abuse.

The Protection for Persons Reporting Child Abuse Act 1998 has probably achieved an appropriate balance between societal desire to protect vulnerable children on the one hand and ensuring one's constitutional right to protection of one's good name from unjust attack on the other.[107] Additionally there is the right to fair procedures which is well recognised under procedural Irish constitutional law. Section 5 created a new criminal offence of false reporting of child abuse ensuring the discouragement of malicious reports where the reporter knows the statement to be false. One of the anomalies of this aspect of the legislation is that it is a criminal offence to make a false report of child abuse to a designated officer but it would not be an offence if made to a non-designated officer. In drafting this legislation the temptation to tilt the balance in favour of children was avoided by the legislation. Glendenning has noted that teachers in Irish schools welcome this legislation as relevant to the school setting 'as teachers previously felt particularly vulnerable when reporting any form of child abuse'.[108]

9. Guidelines on Child Abuse

> *So is it appropriate to sound a great hurrah now because Ireland is finally introducing child protection guidelines just in time to beat the 31 December 1999 deadline?*
> M. Ruane, The Irish Times, 27 September 1999

In September 1999, the Irish Department of Health and Children published additional guidelines for dealing with child abuse which significantly updated earlier versions of those guidelines. Prior to 1999, the Department of Health issued the only reportage guidelines that existed: 'Notification of Suspected Cases of Child Abuse between Health Boards and Gardaí, 1995.' Prior to these, the 1987 Department of Health 'Guidelines on Procedures for the Identification, Investigation and Management of Child Abuse' applied. Essentially the latest guidelines, which fall short of a regime of mandatory reporting,[109] nevertheless represent an authentic attempt at establishing a national and local system for reporting abuse. Entitled *Children First: National Guidelines for the Protection and Welfare of Children* (1999), the guidelines were drafted by a Working Group originally established in February 1998.[110] This 165-page report recommended, *inter alia*, that the Report should be the 'national guidelines which are applied consistently by all health boards, governments and organisations providing services to children. Consideration should be given to this requirement being put on a statutory basis.' The Terms of Reference of the Working Group were to review:

   (i)   guidelines on procedures for the identification, investigation and management of child abuse; and

  (ii) notification of suspected cases of child abuse between Health Boards and Gardaí; and

 (iii) to prepare revised guidelines aimed at improving the identification, investigation and management of child abuse.

The *Children First Report* (1999) was a clear acknowledgement that the profile of child abuse as a social problem had risen considerably in Ireland and was urgently in need of a structured, centralised, socio-legal response. At the launch of the Guidelines, Mr Frank Fahey, then junior Minister for Health and Children, indicated that 'these guidelines would act as overarching guidelines that applied to all individuals and agencies who have contact with children'. Essentially the guidelines apply nationally but especially to institutional bodies and professional practitioners within the child care contexts. The earlier child abuse guidelines were regularly criticised for not being uniformly implemented within the eight Health Board regions.

McElwee has recently noted that:

> . . . there has been an overemphasis on child sexual
> abuse during the latter part of the decade at the expense
> of other forms of abuse such as emotional abuse and
> neglect.[111]

The new guidelines profess to be informed by the principles underlying the Child Care Act 1991 and the UNCRC, specifically that the child's welfare is paramount, but also to have regard to the needs of families and to the child's wishes. The central objective of the guidelines is to facilitate professionals in identifying and reporting child abuse primarily to the respective Health Boards and to An Garda Síochána. The term 'abuse' has been given an expansive and flexible meaning. 'Abuse' is classified within four circumstances, i.e. neglect, emotional abuse, physical abuse and finally sexual abuse, with prominence however given to the particular problems associated with *neglect*. 'Neglect' is defined in terms of *omission* 'where the child suffers significant harm or impairment of development by being deprived of food, clothing, warmth, hygiene, intellectual stimulation, supervision and safety, attachment to and affection from adults, medical care. Child abuse within an 'emotional' context is not one which Irish society has traditionally regarded as coming within the normal understanding of child abuse. Emotional abuse is now defined as an 'abuse which is found primarily within the relationship between caregiver and a child and occurs when a child's need for affection, approval, consistency and security are not met'. The standard paradigmatic notion of child abuse, i.e. physical abuse, is defined as 'any form of non-accidental injury or injury which results from wilful or neglectful failure to protect a child'. Child sexual abuse is defined as that occurring when 'a child is used by another person for his or her gratification or sexual arousal or for that of others'. However, the Working Group regarded this as not a legal definition, and it was not intended to be a description of the criminal offences of sexual assault.

The designated persons for reporting of abuse are similar to those under the Protection for Persons Reporting Child Abuse Act 1998. For bodies associated with children, clear written procedures must be implemented when allegations of abuse are made against employees or volunteers. All abuse reports must be treated seriously by the Health Boards and the abuse complaint must be evaluated. Health Boards are required to treat seriously every abuse report, from minor to major, and are obliged to examine with due care each complaint including those made anonymously. In Ireland, social workers have occasionally been judicially criticised for not being familiar with the abuse guidelines which should inform their work practices at a particular time. In *GF v. AF* (1995) District Judge William Early was severely critical of the failure of some professionals to comply with the prescribed procedures to investigate and validate allegations of child sexual abuse in a custody/access case brought under the Guardianship of Infants Act 1964. In this case the mother alleged that the father of the child had sexually abused their daughter. Referring to the Department of Health's abuse guidelines at the time, the district judge suggested that these publications should be known and, more importantly, should be adhered to by all persons involved in the investigation and assessment of cases of child sexual abuse. On the alleged inadequacy of Irish social workers/child care practitioners, Dr Buckley (TCD) states that:

> While Ireland has not yet experienced a backlash akin to that precipitated by the 'Cleveland crisis' in the UK there are certainly examples of where individual practitioners have been deemed overzealous in their diagnosis of child sexual abuse and have been the subject of legal action as a consequence.[112]

In essence therefore these guidelines represent a conscious policy and practice of updating, in a protective manner, the understanding of the principal types of child abuse and how to recognise it. Standard reporting procedures are stipulated in detail which is possibly the most important provision in the guidelines overall. The implication for professionals and the public at large is that any person who suspects that a child is being abused, or is at risk of abuse, should make a report to the Health Board or the police. The core maxim is that everyone now has a duty to protect children and reports should be made to the statutory authorities without delay. Furthermore, the guidelines provide principled, practical, clear and powerful criteria for various organisations on the reporting mechanism to be adopted, requiring each to appoint a designated person to act as a liaison with outside agencies. Among the sixteen recommendations made by the twenty-one-member Working Group was the need to see guidelines implemented on an inter-agency and inter-disciplinary level with concomitant collaboration and communication at national and local levels. A comprehensive programme of training in child protection was also advocated as well as a public information campaign to promote positive parenting, an awareness of child abuse and the existence of the guidelines.

What then is the net effect of these guidelines for Irish children's rights generally? They should make Ireland a safer place for children to actualise their potential as they make their way towards adulthood. They represent the benchmarks in child protection policy. Although the guidelines do not constitute a panacea, they nevertheless remove any practice or principle uncertainty as to what should be done when there is reason to suspect that a child is being neglected or emotionally, physically or sexually abused. Certainly no professional social worker, child care personnel or police officer can legitimately argue credibly that they did not know what to do when confronted with a child abuse scenario. The guidelines also affirm the statutory responsibility of Health Boards to provide support services to the families of children who may be at risk of abuse or neglect. They offer guidance on the delivery of family support services including assessment and preparation of family support plans and agreements. This child care strategy acknowledges the need for an approach which primarily and necessarily respects the need for a balance between the socio-legal rights of families and those of children. In other words, the guidelines expressly state when children are to be proactively protected by the State, through the statutory bodies, and when families must also be supported in order to do their best by their children.

The existence of those guidelines will therefore act as a pressure on the State to provide the requisite funding. There will also be pressure on the Health Boards to utilise their child care personnel to maximum effect. Although not legally binding, the guidelines nevertheless represent political determination 'to take greater cognisance of the needs of children generally in our society and of the impact of various decisions by [the Irish] Government on children's lives'.[113] The guidelines probably represent the first step in articulating publicly a formally recognised contract with Ireland's children that as citizens of the nation they will get immediate protection, not according to adult and institutional time but according to children's time, which is the present.

Children are not adults-in-waiting, for they cannot wait for their rights. Institutional structural changes will inevitably be necessary in such Irish Government Departments as Health and Children; Justice, Equality and Law Reform; Education, Science and Technology and, finally, the various Health Boards. Given the structural fragmentation on children's issues in Ireland it is imperative that external auditing be undertaken to supervise the supervisors (Health Boards and Gardaí).

10. Child Poverty in Ireland

There is a certain incongruity about the coexistence of a booming Irish economy and the continued existence of a significant level of child poverty in Ireland. Recent research from the Combat Poverty Agency (CPA), which focused exclusively on the theme of 'child poverty' in Ireland, revealed that the level of child poverty was exceptionally high in Ireland and that a substantial gap had opened between poverty rates for children and those of adults.[114] It seems that the issue of child poverty is moving inexorably to the centre of public policy matters at both the European and national levels. Ms Diamantopoulou, the EU Commissioner for Social Affairs, has recently proposed a European target for the reduction of child poverty by at least 50 per cent before 2010. In February 2000, Mr Dermot Ahern, Minister for Social, Community and Family Affairs, told an EU Council of Labour and Social Affairs that, given the Irish Government's particular concern at the levels of Irish child poverty, he was examining the possibility of setting a target for the reduction of child poverty as part of the National Anti-Poverty Strategy.

The recent findings of the CPA give serious cause for concern. Firstly, Ireland fares quite badly when compared with other EU member states, in that Ireland has the highest national rate of child poverty of any EU member state. Portugal and the UK were the only EU members to have nearly as high a rate. A report from UNICEF Ireland (2000) reveals that the proportion of children living below the poverty line in the Republic of Ireland was more than twice that in the Netherlands and France and more than six times that of some Scandinavian countries. Hugh Frazer, Director of the Combat Poverty Agency, summarised the implications of this crucial point when he stated that:

> . . . in 1997 a quarter of Irish children were still poor and around one in six were in severe and consistent poverty . . . a very large number of children are still growing up experiencing poverty. In an affluent society like ours this is unacceptable. It undermines the well-being of children and limits their basic rights. It also undermines their development and future life chances. Poor children are more likely to suffer poor health, to do less well educationally and to be at risk of crime and anti-social behaviour.[115]

The second major finding of the CPA was that in 1997 one in four children lived in households of below half the average income. As a means of remedying this significant disadvantage for Irish children the CPA has recommended a set of policy proposals for promoting the welfare of children and ending child poverty. These cover:

- Strengthening the rights of children in our laws, policies and practices;
- Developing a co-ordinated strategy to tackle child poverty;
- Enhancing public subvention of children;
- Combating discrimination and ensuring equal opportunity for all children.

The most recent research indicates that there is a very gradual decrease in child poverty levels in Ireland. Nolan's *Child Poverty in Ireland Report* (July 2000) found that fewer Irish children live in poverty than six years ago, primarily because of growth in the number of people at work.[116] The proportion of children living in poverty fell from 29 per cent in 1994 to 26 per cent in 1997, the latest year on which this Report's figures are based. It is highly likely that a further improvement has taken place since then. Despite this fall, however, 170,000 Irish children are growing up in poverty. As an immediate response to this scandalous situation, Nolan's Report recommended that child benefit payments should be more than doubled as a key component of an attack on child poverty. The forgotten statistic about child poverty is that children of immigrants and asylum seekers are also affected by poverty in all sorts of ways. Of course it would be naive to think that child poverty could be tackled in isolation. Therefore, targeting child poverty itself needs to be located within a broader societal strategy to improve in a quantifiable way the well-being of Irish children. Taking an even broader macro view, the elimination of Irish child poverty in Ireland must inevitably involve other public policy programmes for the advancement of the economic, social, cultural, civil and political rights of children. The slogan used in the recent media campaign to highlight child poverty is apt:

Let's end child poverty. We can well afford it.

The *Irish Independent*, 21 June 2000, had an extraordinary headline in relation to one aspect of child poverty: 'Taoiseach backs school meals for children in need'. The idea that children are attending school in this day and age without the basic meals is somewhat alarming. It does not seem to fit comfortably with the image of Ireland of the booming economy. The stated objective of this scheme, according to the Taoiseach, is to provide a basic meals service (breakfast and lunch) in schools in disadvantaged areas to help keep needy children in the education system. Perhaps the time has arrived when less money should be invested in setting up golf courses through the lottery funds. The provision of meals for children is surely a matter of greater urgency than the provision of golf courses. There is something anomalous in a country where there are four times as many golf courses than there are children's playgrounds!

11. Conclusions

Successive Governments almost since the foundation of the State, certainly since the adoption of the Constitution of the 1930s, don't appear to have cared much, if at all, about what the Constitution has had to say about the rights and entitlements of children . . . in good times and in bad, in eras of prosperity and of hardship, the State has consistently turned its back on . . . children.

Editorial, The Irish Times, 18 April 2000

In Ireland concern is expressed periodically about the content and possible amendments of the Constitution of Ireland. On such issues as divorce and abortion there have been divisive national debates in which many sections of Irish society became somewhat agitated about the subject matter of the proposed referenda. The recommendation of the *Report of the Constitution Review Group* (1996) regarding the insertion of express children's rights into an amended and significantly extended Article 41 of the Irish Constitution has not resulted in any major upsurge of demand for such a constitutional referendum. There has never really been a national debate or national forum to debate the issue of the place of children's rights in our society. Even the notion of codifying or consolidating the various judicial determinations on child law from the superior Irish Courts has not found favour as one possible conflict-free route towards establishing a children's rights legal base in Ireland. In November 1999, a Private Members' Bill, the *Twenty-First Amendment of the Constitution (No. 5) Bill 1999*, was introduced into the Dáil by the Labour Party, which sought to amend Article 41 of the Constitution by the addition of the following subsection:

> The State guarantees in its laws to respect, and, as far as practicable, by its laws to defend and vindicate the rights of the child, having regard to international legal standards and in particular to the United Nations Convention on the Rights of the Child, which rights shall include:
>   i. the right to have his or her best interests regarded as the first and paramount consideration in any decision concerning the child;
> ii. the right to know the identity of his or her parents and as far as practicable to be reared by his or her parents, subject to such limitations as may be prescribed by law in the interests of the child; and
> iii. the right to have due regard given to his or her views in any decision concerning the child.[117]

As with most Private Members' Bills, this Bill cannot progress and become law without Governmental approval. The Government in power nearly always opposes a Private Members' Bill, which consequently has little chance of passing even its second stage in Parliament. Nevertheless, its introduction is an indication of the current climate and topicality of children's rights in Ireland.

Perhaps the future prospect of the incorporation of the 1950 European Convention on Human Rights (ECHR) offers another ground for optimism regarding the expansion of the scope and legitimacy of children's rights. Incorporation will therefore have major ramifications for family law in general and for the development of children's rights in particular. Incorporation will also necessarily result in an additional body of laws which will have as their objective the promotion and protection of children's rights in both the private and public spheres. Ireland was one of the first countries to ratify the Convention in 1953, yet it is one of the few not to have already incorporated it into its domestic legislation. On 18 April 2000 the Irish Cabinet indicated its intention of incorporating the Convention into Irish law by way of special legislation rather than by referendum. Consequently, in terms of hierarchy of law in our legal system, whilst it will coexist with the other sources of Irish law, in the event of a clash between the Convention and the Irish Constitution, the former must yield to the latter. Litigants will be able to cite the Convention as well as its body of case law in Irish courts.

The principal Convention rights affecting public and private child law are Articles 6 (fair hearing and trial), Article 8 (right to respect for family life) and Article 14 (prohibition of discrimination). Indeed the majority of Convention cases concerning family law have involved children's issues with most of those cases involving public law issues, such as the interference by a public authority with an individual's 'right to respect for his family life', resulting in the removal of children from their families with consequential determinations relating to placement of children with other carers. Private law cases are less susceptible to regulation by the organs of the Convention because disputes between parents and other carers and relatives will usually involve the State only if the application has been made to Court. Children's private lives are especially protected under Article 8, which states that:

1. Everyone has the right to respect for his private and family life, his home and his correspondence.
2. There shall be no interference by a public authority with the exercise of this right except such as is in accord with the law and is necessary in a democratic society in the interests of national security . . .

Arising from this Article, children's rights now encompass respect for their 'family life' and respect for their 'private life'. Essentially, where familial life is deemed to exist, the child of the family is entitled in his or her own right to respect for his or her 'family life'. A child also enjoys protection in his or her private life, which includes such factors as the moral and physical integrity of the particular child. Ursula Kilkelly's recent academic study on the impact of the Convention on child law indicates that wherever family life is found to be in existence, each of the family members will, independently, be entitled to respect for their family life. [118] It would appear, however, that the Convention does not expressly provide that the rights of children are paramount. To date, the European Court of Human Rights gives each family member the right of respect for his or her private life and family life in equal weight and then determines to what extent, if at all, the individual rights of each family member are in conflict. Swindells concludes that: 'The welfare of the child becomes relevant then only when the Court comes to consider whether interference with the rights of family members is justified as necessary . . .' [119]

It is imperative that all children living in the Republic of Ireland do not become victims of tokenism and hypocrisy when it comes to children's rights. Since the late 1990s, Irish Governments have attempted to give more than mere lip service to both the letter and the spirit of the UNCRC. This is so in spite of the absence of a Government commitment regarding the possibility or feasibility of ever incorporating this prestigious and persuasive international Convention into Irish law. If the letter or the spirit of the UNCRC is to be taken seriously, it will cost a great amount of money to implement. Children's economic, social and cultural rights have a cost implication and will inevitably involve a shift in the current allocation of resources away from present social spending programmes, which exclude children, to specific programmes which include children's issues. Child legislation will founder if resourced inadequately. In this context Professor Freeman's comments regarding the under-resourcing of child law is apt.

> Children's rights without services are meaningless, and services without resources cannot be provided.[120]

The possibility of imposing higher taxes in order to establish and/or develop children's rights would not be popular with most Irish taxpayers who are currently enjoying the full benefits of the boom of the 'Celtic Tiger' economy. If children's rights are going to cost, what then is the approach to be adopted if Irish society is reluctant and unwilling to fund them, especially if they involve a concomitant higher tax burden? Given this economic reality, it is strategically wiser for advocates of children's rights, such as the NGOs, to continue their well-funded drive towards educating the public at large about children's rights in Ireland. On the issue of whether politicians regard children's rights as a matter of economic priority, one Canadian study has noted that:

> Direct pressure upon governments is not likely to result in greater resources devoted to children unless the governments themselves are convinced that any reallo-cation is politically sustainable. In the interim, lower cost initiatives should be advanced, which are likely to capture the public imagination and to build interest in children's issues.[121]

Whilst there is an acknowledged fragmentation of approach by various Government Departments towards children's issues generally, there is no deliberate inertia or evasiveness in attempt-ing to tackle the not insurmountable problems in the child law area. It may smack of tokenism to some commentators to have a mere junior Minister of State, who is without Cabinet status, responsible for children's issues. The current Minister of State for Children, Ms Mary Hanafin, has adopted a high-profile approach towards improving the everyday lives of children similar to that of her predecessor, Mr Frank Fahey. Her Department is currently drawing up a ten-year *National Children's Strategy* (NCS), which will form the basis for the Government's action plan for children. The NCS will have measurable goals, objectives and time frames. It must inevitably try and put in place institutional structures as a means of ensuring a more coherent co-ordination of children's policies, services and practices. Early indications point to the conclusion that the NCS will avoid vague language and will attempt to steer clear of providing a litany of aspirations. The NCS, according to Minister Hanafin, will:

> . . . make a significant contribution to our efforts for children. The Strategy will provide a vision of what we want as a society to achieve for our children over the next ten years. We are now a confident and well-educated people with a successful economy, and we must use these resources to help those less advantaged, particularly children. They must be our first concern, as they are our future. The challenge of the National Children's Strategy is to be fully inclusive and to address the issue of marginalisation . . . The Strategy . . . will ensure that this new millennium is one of hope for all children.[122]

The fundamental problem at the political level, however, is that children's issues cannot easily be accommodated within one well-defined single Government portfolio. Matters concerning children cross various Departments. If 'child-proofing' of all legislation is to be adopted as best practice then all Government Departments will have to develop systems for implementing that policy. More sophisticated statistics on children's issues are needed in order to monitor the impact of social policies on vulnerable and disadvantaged children. The recent establishment of the Courts Service (1999) has already resulted in an array of statistics being available on civil and criminal law matters associated with children. In February 2000, a new Advisory Body on child care was set up to advise Ministers on residential care for children who have behavioural problems, who are in trouble with the law, or who are 'out of control'.

Since 1997, under Section 23 of the Non-Fatal Offences Against the Person Act, it is now possible for children over the age of 16 to give their own autonomous consent to 'any surgical, medical or dental treatment' without the necessity of also obtaining the consent of parent or guardian. Section 24 of this Act adds further to the cluster of children's rights which, if viewed in isolation, is minor but, when viewed collectively with other minor rights, enhances to a certain degree the legal status of children. This section of the Non-Fatal Offences Against the Person Act 1997, which abolished the common law rule in respect of immunity of teachers from criminal liability for punishing pupils, states that:

> The rule of law under which teachers are immune from criminal liability in respect of physical chastisement of pupils is hereby abolished.

Teachers who now physically chastise pupils may be found guilty of a criminal offence and therefore liable to imprisonment for twelve months or a fine not exceeding £1,500 or both. In January 1999, a Limerick primary school teacher was the first person to be convicted under the 1997 Act for pulling a pupil's hair as well as striking him on the back of the head. At a minimum, this legislation protects the dignity and bodily integrity of all school-going children during their years in school. Under the Education Act 1998, there are some provisions which will for the first time give children in schools the statutory right to have their opinions and voices heard within the context of Student Councils. Although not yet commenced, Section 27 (3) to (5) stipulates the nature and scope of these Student Councils at the post-primary level. School Boards are mandatorily obliged to encourage the establishment by students of a Student Council and are also obliged to facilitate and give all reasonable assistance to students who wish to establish one. The sole objective of the Student Council is to promote the interests of the school and the involvement of students in the affairs of the school, in co-operation with the School Board, parents and teachers. A Student Council may also make rules governing its meetings and the business and conduct of its affairs. This institutional structure for children's voices to be heard will encounter some opposition from teachers who must adjust psychologically to the situation that children have a right to be heard. Other teachers are anxious about the effect that these councils will have on the pupil-teacher relationship and the balance of power in that relationship. One thing is certain, however, and that is that the absolute authoritarianism previously enjoyed by Irish teachers must now yield to a more comprehensive understanding of the rights of children in schools. One might ask why the voices of primary school children are not being heard through the medium of a Student Council for each primary school.

Perhaps in the final analysis, the establishment of a 'Commissioner for Children' or a 'Children's Ombudsman' (the terms are used here interchangeably) will provide a most significant independent institutional mechanism through which Irish children and young people can be heard and affirmed.[123] The existence of such an Office within our political structures will represent a manifest expression of Irish society's authentic commitment to recognise and respect children's rights and to be held accountable on that commitment. Since children have no political voice it is therefore all the more imperative that they be provided with an effective medium whereby their rights can be highlighted, protected and implemented. With all the freedom, autonomy and authority of the Office, the Commissioner for Children will 'tell it like it is and as it ought to be', thus providing a responsive forum which will give value and relevance to children who to date have been a voiceless and powerless minority in Irish society.

In their *Concluding Observations Report* in Geneva (January 1998) the UN Committee on the Rights of the Child expressed their concern about the lack of an independent monitoring mechanism such as a Children's Ombudsman. Their Report exhorted the Irish Government to consider positively the establishment of such an Office. In 1996 the Council of Europe's Parliamentary Assembly recommended that Member States should establish a Commissioner for Children. The Children's

Ombudsman can tentatively be defined as an investigator or neutral factfinder of children's legitimate problems and complaints. The Commissioner would act as a catalyst for change in order to advance the welfare and best interests of children. The essential hallmark of the paradigm for a Children's Commissioner is that the office-holder should be comparatively unconstrained by political interference and free to challenge government legislation, policy and resource commitments to children's issues. What model of Ombudsman then is most appropriate for this jurisdiction? Essentially there are at least three possible options available for establishing the office of a Children's Ombudsman. These are:

(a) Constitutional Children's Ombudsman;

(b) Non-Statutory Administrative Model; and

(c) Statutory Model.

After lengthy consultations by the Department of Health and Children with academics, child care practitioners, lawyers, NGOs and Children's Ombudspersons in other jurisdictions (i.e. Norway and New Zealand), it seems likely that Ireland will opt for the statutory model. Nevertheless it is worth considering briefly the advantages and disadvantages associated with the other two models. The significant advantage of the constitutional model is that the Children's Commissioner would be placed on a lofty constitutional pedestal similar to that of the Comptroller and Auditor General. This would necessitate a constitutional amendment, requiring the Government to publish in advance the various arguments for and against the proposal. Given the interpretive complexities of the Irish Constitution in relation to the privileging of the autonomy of the marital family as a social unit, as stated in Article 41, any amendment which involved a Commissioner for Children regulating and/or monitoring children's rights would necessarily need to be compatible with and in harmony with Articles 41 and 42 of the Constitution.

The establishment of a non-statutory Commissioner for Children by means of an Administrative, Ministerial or Executive Order or Directive is a second possible model, but it has significant and fatal disadvantages. If appointed by a Government Minister, this person would report directly and be accountable to the relevant Minister. Inevitably therefore, the office-holder would not be able to operate independently and effectively if ministerial interference were a regular occurrence. She/he could be dismissed without much legal difficulty were they, for example, to refuse to terminate an investigation which the Minister might deem inappropriate. Reporting to a Government Minister might also not be a guarantee that that the Minister would publish either the annual report or a report on a particular matter.

On 26 July 1999 Carol Coulter, the *Irish Times* legal affairs correspondent, wrote that the 'Government is to appoint Ombudsman for Children . . . and is likely to be a reality in 2000'. The model that is to be adopted by the current Government is the statutory one, which will contain the overall terms of reference and conditions, which will determine the numerous powers and duties that are necessary for the proper functioning of the Office. The legislation must delineate and define the parameters of the investigative procedures, as well as the precise authority, which the office-holder has for addressing children's issues. It is essential that the Children's Ombudsman must possess the power to investigate, to report, to criticise and to indicate how a child-related matter should be dealt with and to recommend a specified remedial action and/or a change in practice to avoid a recurrence. There must be no doubt about the independent and autonomous nature of the Office. Allied to this, appropriate funding, staffing and general resourcing must be provided exclusively by the Oireachtas at an agreed level necessary for the maximum efficiency of the Office. Any diminution of funding or staffing could be interpreted as an attack on the impartiality and independence of the Office, given that the quantity and quality of staffing and budget can determine the effectiveness and strength of the Office.

If the legislation is to have credibility, the children's 'watchdog' must have statutory teeth and must be prepared to utilise them effectively as an instrument of redress and socio-political control. It is imperative that the Children's Ombudsman also has rights of access to all public and private institutions as well as rights of access to all documentation in matters concerning children. Other statutory features must include powers to compel persons to attend investigative meetings and rights to be consulted about all legislation affecting children directly and indirectly – the legislation must also endow the office-holder with formidable moral authority. Dismissal or removal must be restricted to those which apply to the judiciary (i.e. 'for stated misbehaviour or incapacity') and this can only be done upon resolution of both Houses of the Oireachtas. This complex dismissal procedure ensures the independence of the Office and facilitates its functioning to the fullest. Howard Davidson of the American Bar Association has noted that:

> Risk of losing a job, or fear of retaliation, will not be in the best interests of the children who depend on the Ombudsman to protect their interests.[124]

Appointment and tenure should be limited to a term of five years renewable once. It is generally acknowledged that the 'burnout' rate for Children's Ombudspersons is quite high. The annual or special Reports are the weapons of the Children's Ombudsman and underpin his/her moral authority and persuasiveness. Through these Reports, children's issues are highlighted sometimes to the embarrassment of those who may be unco-operative in the Commissioner's investigations. By establishing a Children's Ombudsman, Irish democracy is all the more enhanced. The image of Irish children as appendages and adjuncts of adults is gradually being de-emphasised and replaced with the image of children as emerging and developing autonomous citizens. Now more than ever this evolving status requires to be promoted and protected. Who better than the vigilance of a Children's Ombudsman to facilitate this new citizenship? The ultimate aim and objective of the Commissioner for Children is to be put out of work for lack of business. Such an outcome would be devoutly to be desired by all sections of Irish society.

Ireland is now at the crossroads regarding children's rights. Ireland 'could do significantly better'. There is a notable increase in the level of consciousness of children's rights among politicians, administrators and the judiciary who are all beginning to accept, reluctantly however, the simple fact that children are rights-holders and these rights must be promulgated, protected and promoted. Disabled children continue to suffer discrimination particularly in terms of equality of educational opportunity. Child homelessness, begging on the streets and child malnutrition are issues that need to be addressed without delay. Corporal punishment of children within the family home still exists with no effort being made to declare it illegal. Many children are leaving school illiterate after years of formal education. School suspensions and school expulsions of pupils continue without sufficient consideration to the due process rights of these children. If Irish society is to take children's rights seriously then more effective methods must be developed for enforcing those rights. The establishment of a Government Ministry for Children in Ireland would be one more overt manifestation that we are taking children's rights seriously.

Notes

1   J. Fortin, *Children's Rights and the Developing Law* (London: Butter-worths, 1998), p. 13.

2   Perez de Cuellar, UN Secretary General, Legnano, Italy, September 1987.

3   P. Cullen, *Refugees and Asylum Seekers in Ireland* (Cork University Press, 2000), p. 1.

4   See UNHCR, *Guidelines on Refugee Children*, 1988; *Guidelines on Protection and Care*, 1994.

5   B.B. Woodhouse, 'Child Custody in an Age of Children's Rights', *Family Law Quarterly*, Autumn 1999, vol. 3, p. 815.

6   *Convention on the Rights of the Child*, GA Res. 44/25, 44 GAOR Supp. (No. 49) p. 165, UN DOC A/44 736.

7   M. Freeman (ed.), *Children's Rights: A Comparative Perspective* (Dart-mouth, Ashgate, 1996), p. 4. See generally G. van Bueren, *The International Law on the Rights of the Child* (The Hague: Martinus Nijhoff, 1995).

8   *Concluding Observations of the Committee on the Rights of the Child: Ireland*, UN Committee on the Rights of the Child, 17th Session, UN DOC CRC/C/15 Add. 85, (23 January 1998). For a contrastive report and analysis see *Concluding Observations of the Committee on the Rights of the Child: United Kingdom of Great Britain and Northern Ireland*, UN Committee on the Rights of the Child, 8th Session, UN DOC CRC/C/15 Add. 34, (1995). For an evaluation of New Zealand's Compliance Report see *Concluding Observations on New Zealand's Initial Report*, CRC/C/15 Add. 71, (24 January 1997).

9   See generally P. Ward, *The Child Care Act 1991* (Dubli: Round Hall, 1995). Also, H. Ferguson and P. Kenny, *On Behalf of the Child* (Dublin: Farmar, 1995).

10 *First National Compliance Report of Ireland* (Department of Foreign Affairs, Government Publications Office, Dublin, 1996), p. 5.

11 UN *Concluding Observations*, p. 2, paras 4 and 24.

12 S. Kilbourne, 'The Wayward American – Why the USA has not ratified the UNCRC', *Child and Family Law Quarterly* 10 (1998), p. 243.

13 UNICEF, *The State of the World's Children* (New York: 1990), p. 11.

14 A. Bainham and C. Cretney, *Children: The Modern Law* 2nd edn. (Bristol: Jordans, 1998), p. 59. Prevention applies to Articles 2, 11 and 24. Protection applies to Article 37. Provision applies to Articles

27–29 and 31. Finally, Participation applies to Articles 12, 13 and 17.

15   J. Goldstein, A. Freud, and A. Solnit, A.J., *Beyond the Best Interests of the Child* (New York: The Free Press, 1973), p. 13.

16   Kilbourne, 1998, p. 245.

17   For a critical evaluation of 'The Family' in the Irish Constitution (Article 41), see F. Martin 'The Family in the Irish Constitution: Principle and Practice', in Murphy and Twomey (eds.), *Ireland's Evolving Constitution, 1937–1997: Collected Essays* (Oxford: Hart Publishing, 1998), pp. 79–95. See also A. Shatter, *Family Law* 4th edn. (Dublin: Butterworths, 1997), especially pp. 5–43. For an extensive analysis of children's education rights in Ireland, see D. Glendenning, *Education and the Law* (Dublin: Butterworths, 1999).

18   W. Duncan, 'Hague Conference on Private International Law and The Children's Conventions', 2, *Irish Journal of Family Law*, (1998), p. 5. The Hague Conference's website at *http://www.hcch.net.* See also A. Hutchinson and M. Bennett, 'The Hague Child Protection Convention 1996', *Family Law*, January [1998], 35.

19   Bainham, 1998 p. 57. For an account of this adverse reaction see F. Martin, 'UN Critical of Ireland's Child Poverty Strategies', *Poverty Today*, January 1999, p. 20.

20   Van Bueren, 1995, p. 413.

21   U. Kilkelly, *Small Voices: Vital Rights* (Dublin: Children's Rights Alliance, 1997) pp. 1–2. This 62-page publication was the Alliance's formal NGO submission to the UN Committee on the Rights of the Child in response to the Government's 1996 Compliance Report.

22   See *First National Compliance Report of Ireland,* 1996, p. 116.

23   See Kilkelly, 1997.

24   For a brief account of the pre-sessional meeting, see *Children's Rights: Our Responsibilities* (Dublin: Children's Rights Alliance, 1998).

25   W. Duncan, 'The Constitutional Protection of Parental Rights', p. 431 in J. Eekelaar and P. Sarcevic (eds.), *Parenthood in Modern Society* (The Hague: Martinus Nijhoff, 1993).

26   For a view of the welfare principle in the UK, see Davis/Pearse, 'On the Trail of the Welfare Principle', *Family Law* [1999] 14. See generally W. Duncan, 'The Child, the Parent and the State; the Balance of Power' in *Law and Social Policy* (TCD, 1987).

27   [1996] 2 IR 248.

28 [1994] ILRM, 126, 132–133.

29 Kilkenny Incest Investigation Report (Dublin: Government Publications, May 1993, Pl. 9812), p. 96.

30 [1996] 2 IR 20. The child in this case was profoundly mentally and physically disabled. The unusual jurisprudential feature of the case is that it is one of the first superior Court judgments which directly refers to the text of the UNCRC, in particular Articles 2, 23, 28 and 29.

31 P. Tapp, 'The United Nations Convention on the Rights of the Child – The First Decade'. In the recent landmark High Court judgement of *Sinnott v. Minister for Education* (HC), UNREP, October 2000, Justice Barr affirmed the *O'Donoghue* (1996) principle that a severely disabled person is constitutionally entitled to free primary education which the State must provide. *New Zealand Law Review*, (1999) 453, p. 455. For three New Zealand cases which applied the UNCRC see, *G. v. N.* (F.C. Wanganui, FPO83/363/97, 9 June 1999, Judge Walsh); *N. v. A.* (D.C. Auckland, FPOO4/975/95, 25 June 1999, Judge Doogue) and *The Queen v. F* (H.C.Auckland, T 982638, 22 June 1999, Laurenson J).

32 [1991] 1 ILRM 93, 95. For a brief overview of this case, and other similar cases, see T. Blake, 'Child Protection and Welfare while in Care: the Role of the Courts', *Bar Review*, October 1998, pp. 12–14.

33 ibid. at pp. 103–5. Justice Kelly at p. 100 examined the parameters of a child's constitutional right and concluded that: 'It is one which is limited by time because it can be enjoyed by a citizen only whilst a minor.' See P. Ward, 'Children: Detention and Abortion' in A. Bainham (ed.) *The International Survey of Family Law 1997*, (The Hague: Martinus Nijhoff, 1999), pp. 355–377. An analogous legal and factual judgment with a not dissimilar outcome was given by Kelly, J. *TD (a minor) v. Minister for Education (ex tempore)* in 4 December 1998.

34 Ward, Ibid. pp. 362–3. Justice Kelly's reprimand of the Executive branch of Government resulted in an immediate response from the Department of Health and Children approving proposals to build more than treble the number of high-support and secure residential places for such children by 2000. Kelly J. regarded the proposals as representing 'the Department's Herculean efforts to meet the needs of vulnerable children'. See *The Irish Times*, 15 April 1999.

35 Section 47 of the Child Care Act 1991 states that: 'Where a child is in the care of the Health Board, the District Court may, of its own motion or on an application of any person give such directions and make such order on any question affecting the welfare of the child

as it thinks proper and may vary or discharge any such direction or order.'

36   For one of the latest Irish Supreme Court's jurisprudential statements on children's rights see *Eastern Health Board v. MK*, Unreported Supreme Court, 29 January 1999, especially Denham J.'s judgment, pp. 15–17.

37   P. Ward, 'Care Orders and Judicial Control', *Family Law* April [2000] 285.

38   ibid., p. 286.

39   J. Roche, 'Children's Rights: A Lawyer's View', in M. John (ed.), *Children in our Charge. The Child's Right to Resources* (London: Jessica Kingsley, 1996), p. 24.

40   *DB v. The Minister for Justice* [1999] 1 IR 29, 35.

41   Unreported High Court, 25 February 2000. Kelly, J., at p. 29.

42   J. Fortin, 1998, p. 483.

43   *Report of the Constitution Review Group* (Dublin: Stationery Office, May 1996), Pn. 2632, p.x.

44   For the full Schedule of Documents supplied see *Compliance Report*, 1996, pp.123–4.

45   Ch. 12, pp. 319–37. Two of the Appendices of the Report dealt with Family and Child law issues: Appendix 22, W. Duncan, 'The Constitutional Protection of Parental Rights', pp. 612–26 and Appendix 23, K. Lynch, 'Defining the Family and Protecting the Caring Functions of Traditional and Non-traditional Families', pp. 627–9.

46   Kilkelly, 1997, p.10.

47   Kilkelly, 1997, para. 24. *The Constitution Review Group's Report* was discussed at length during the formal hearing of Ireland's *Compliance Report* on 12 January 1998 in Geneva. See *Summary Record*: Ireland, 436th meeting, CRC/C/SR. 436 especially paras. 27, 32, 37, 46, 68, 83 and 84.

48   Constitution Report, 1996, p.319. Like the US Constitution, the Irish Constitution is regarded both in form and in substance as a 'rigid' constitution particularly in relation to the complexities associated with the amending process. Articles 46–47 regulate the two-stage amendment process.

49   [1998] 2 IR 321, 380–1.

50   The Irish Law Reform Commission *Report on Illegitimacy* (LRC 4 – 1982), p. 88, noted the 'substantial opposition to conferring automatic rights on all fathers of children born outside marriage'.

51   For a comparable judicial discussion on the nature and legal scope of

a child-father relationship see also, *GW v. DJ and Ors*, Unreported, High Court, May 1992, J. O'Hanlon.

52 A. Shatter, 1997, p.1008.

53 See Registration of Births Act (Commencement) Order 1997 (S.I. 45/1997). See generally Births and Deaths Registration Acts 1863–1994. See also Guardianship of Infants Act 1964, S 6A (3) as inserted by the Status of Children Act 1987, S. 12.

54 Most provisions of the Children Act 1997 came into force on 9 January 1999. Children Act 1997 (Commencement Orders), 1998 (S.I. 433/1998). Only two sections are not currently in force, namely Section 26 (as inserted into the Guardianship of Infants Act 1964) which relates to the ordering of social reports in District Court proceedings in matters concerning the welfare of children. More alarming from an empowerment of children's rights perspective is the non-commencement of Section 28 (as inserted into the 1964 Act) providing for the appointment of a guardian *ad litem* in private law proceedings if it is necessarily in the best interests of the child.

55 For a socio-legal analysis of the changing nature of the Irish father-child relationship see generally, K. McKeown, H. Ferguson and D. Rooney in *Changing Fathers*, (Cork: Collins Press 1998) especially Chapter 6, pp. 155–94.

56 [1991] 2 All E R 185.

57 See also, *Re S (Parental Responsibility) [1995] 2 FLR 648 and Re C and V (minors)(contact and parental responsibility) [1998]* 1 FLR 52.

58 G. Shannon, 'Seen but not Heard: Children at Risk in the Legal Process' *Law Society Gazette* (December 1999), pp.19–20.

59 C. Power, 'Practice and Procedure: Children Act 1997 Comes into Force' 1 *Irish Journal of Family Law* [1999], 22.

60 *Final Report of the Commission on the Family, 'Strengthening Families for Life'* (Dublin, Government Publications Office, May 1998).

61 ibid., p. 25.

62 See *Health and Children (Regulation of Ministerial Functions) Order, 1999* (S.I./18 of 1999). The various statutory powers and duties refer to those under (a) the Adoption Acts 1952–1998, (b) the Children Acts 1908–1989 (c) the Child Care Act 1991 and (d) the Protection for Persons Reporting Child Abuse Act, 1998.

63 Section 12, Children Act 1997. See also 480 *Dáil Debates*, Cols. 1328.

64 R. White, P. Carr and N. Lowe, *The Children Act in Practice,* 2nd edn. (London: Butterworths, 1995), p 4. Section 2 (4) of the Children Act

1989, abolished the concept of parental guardianship and the term 'guardian' now only applies to those taking the place of parents upon their death.

65   B. Hoggett, 'The Children Bill: The Aim' *Family Law* [1989], 217. See also B. Hoggett, *Parents and Children*, 4th edn. (Round Hall, Sweet and Maxwell, 1993).

66   For an analysis of the judicial views on the admissibility of children's evidence see *Southern Health Board v CH* [1996] 2 ILRM 142; *In Re M S & W (Infants)* [1996] 1 *ILRM* 370 and *In Re M., S & W (Infants),* Unreported, Supreme Court, 29 January 1999.

67   Guardianship of Children (Statutory Declarations) Regulations 1998 (SI No. 5 1998). For a general review of the Children Act 1997, see P. Ward, *The Children Act 1997*, Irish Current Law Statutes Annotated (Round Hall, Sweet & Maxwell, April 1999). The sworn declaratory parenthood procedure requires the mother and father to declare that they are the father and mother of the child, that the mother agrees to the appointment of the father as guardian of the child and that arrangements are in place regarding custody. Although there is also an option to agree access, the parents are not obliged to recite the precise particulars of the custody/access arrangements.

68   ibid. p. 11. For a brief critique of the Children Act 1997, see R. Ó Riordan, The Children Act 1997, *Bar Review*, June 1999, 371. See *The Irish Times* report of *Dáil Debates* on the Children's Bill, 21 November 1997.

69   [1993] 1 *Family LJ* 34, p. 39.

70   C. Power, 'Practice and Procedure', 1 *IJFL* [1998] 23, 24. See also S.1 No. !25 of 1999 for the practice direction on applications by relatives and those *in loco parentis* for access to a child. For a terse critical comment on the two-stage application process, see C. Power, 'New District Court Rules' 3 *IJFL* [1999] 15. See also M. Martin, 'Third Party Rights of Access to and Custody of Children' 2 *The Bar Review* (1996) 39.

71   In *D v D* [1993] 1 *Family LJ* 34, Carroll J held that a court is entitled to make access orders under the Guardianship of Infants Act 1964 to permit a child access to persons other than its biological parents. Carroll J's view was that access was primarily a child-centred right whereby the emphasis was on the child's access to an adult. For an analysis of the implications of *D v D* (1993) see N.E. Jackson, 'Procedural Matters, Non-Parental Access Rights', 5 *Practice and Procedure*, November 1996, p. 2.

72 The Law Society of Ireland (Solicitors' Profession) have recently called for reform of the child-access orders within the context of familial domestic violence. See *Domestic Violence: The Case for Reform* (Dublin: Law Society of Ireland, 1999).

73 G. Landsdown, 'Key right is the child's right to be heard', 91 *Childright* (1992), p. 4.

74 Section 11 of the Children Act 1997 inserted a new Section 28 of the Guardianship of Infants Act 1964. The net effect of the Children Act 1997 amendment, i.e. the insertion of a new Part IV (Safeguarding Interests of Children), resulted in some significant changes in the Guardianship of Infants Act 1964. with the express objective of improving and safeguarding the interests of children prior to and in the course of private law proceedings under the 1964 Act. However, this provision is not mandatory.

75 In *Re A and B v. Eastern Health Board and the Attorney General* [1998] 1 ILRM 460, *A and B v. Eastern Health Board* [1998] 1 I.R. 464.

76 This provision adheres to the principle underpinning Article 12 (2) of the UNCRC. For an analysis of Guardian *ad litem* in Irish public law proceedings see T. Walsh, 'The Child's Right to Independent Representation: Developments Arising from the Child Care Act 1991; *MLJI* (1997) pp. 66–72.

77 L. O'Sullivan, 'The Guardian *ad litem* in Irish Law – Where Do We Go From Here?, unpublished LL.M. thesis, Winter 1999, National University of Ireland, Cork, p. 42.

78 See generally, C. Corrigan, and C. Forde, *Separate Representation for Children in Ireland.* (Dublin: Coolock Law Centre, 1995). For the latest commentary on possible reform of the English law on a child's legal representation see His Honour Judge N. Fricker QC, 'The New Children and Family Courts Advisory Service', *Family Law,* [February 2000] 102, especially 108.

79 The Sixth Report of the Working Group on a Courts Commission, Pn 6534 (The Denham Report), (Dublin: Government Publications, 1999).

80 On the appointment and functions of English GALs see *The Children Act 1989 Guidance and Regulations Vol. 7, Guardians ad litem and Other Court Related Issues* (London: HMSO, 1991).

81 Section 28 (3) states: 'For the purposes of this section, the court may appoint as a GAL the person from whom, under section 47 (1) of the Act of 1995, a report on any question affecting the welfare of the child

was procured, or such other person as it thinks fit'. See generally, N. Lowe and G. Douglas, *Bromley's Family Law* 9th edn. (Butterworths, 1998), pp. 52–5. Also, S.M. Cretney and J.M. Masson, *Principles of Family Law* 6th edn. (London: Round Hall Sweet & Maxwell, 1997) pp. 597–601 and 829–34. Also, White, Carr and Lowe, 1995, pp. 235–49. See also A. Bainham and C. Cretney, 1998, pp. 446–56.

82   Dublin: Government Publications, 1999 (Pn. 6533), pp. 67–9.

83   Section 64 of the Family Law Act (UK) 1996. For an excellent analysis of the workings of the GAL in England see Head, 'The Work of the Guardian *ad litem*' in K. Wilson and A. James (eds.), *The Child Protection Handbook* (London: Bailliere Tindall, 1995). Head classifies the archetypal duties of the GAL as involving five functions: practical, investigative, analytical, representational and explanatory. See also Ward, 1995, pp. 43–6.

84   Shatter, 1997, p. 643.

85   Law Reform Commission's *Report on Family Courts* (LRC 52 – 1996), p. 112. The Law Society of Ireland's *Family Law in Ireland: Code of Practice* (1995), para. 9.5.

86   See summary of submission by the UK Association of Lawyers for Children to the Lord Chancellor's Advisory Board on Family Law in 'The Future Representation for Children', *Family Law* (July 1998) 403.

87   M. Freeman, 'Taking Children's Rights More Seriously' in P. Alston, S. Parker, J. Seymour, eds., *Children, Rights and the Law* (Oxford: Clarendon Press, 1992), pp. 52–71.

88   ibid., p. 61.

89   For an incisive analysis of the relationship between children and the courts see M. King and C. Piper, *How the Law Thinks about Children* 2nd edn. (Dartmouth: Ashgate, 1995).

90   M. Freeman (1996), p. 5.

91   J. Dewar, 'Concepts, Coherence and Content of Family Law' in Bicks, *Examining the Law Syllabus: Beyond the Core* (Oxford University Press, 1993), p. 81.

92   This theme is analysed by M. Freeman, 'Questioning the Delegalisation Movement in Family Law: Do We Really Want a Family Court?' pp. 7–25, in J. Eekelaar and S. Ketz, (eds.), *The Resolution of Family Conflict: Comparative Legal Perspectives* (London: Butterworths, 1984).

93 *MD v. GD* 1 [1993] *Family L.J.* 34, p. 38. In many senses, Carroll J was prompting such a development, which is now contained in Section 9 of the Children Act 1997. See also M. Martin, 'Third Party Rights of Access to and Custody of Children' 2 *The Bar Review* (1996) 39.

94 See S. 1. No. 125 of District Court (Custody and Guardianship of Children) Rules 1999. This statutory instrument gave effect to the array of legal changes introduced by the Children Act 1997.

95 *The Southern Health Board v. CH* [1996] 2 ILRM 142; [1996] IFLR 101; [1996] 1 IR 219.

96 [1990] ILRM 767; [1991] 1 IR 189.

97 ibid. pp. 200 and 205.

98 ibid. p. 197.

99 [1996] IFLR at p. 117. For other similar statements of O'Flaherty J on the 'best interests/inquiry' judicial approach see *MF v. Superintendent of Ballymun Garda Station* [1991] 1 IR 189, especially p. 202.

100 A. Shatter, 1997, p. 593.

101 The Act came into operation on 23 January 1999, one month after being passed. For a full account of the Act's slow and much opposed passage through parliament see generally 486 *Dáil Debates*, Cols. 906–33 and 1184–207; 493 *Dáil Debates*, Cols. 943–61 and 498 *Dáil Debates*, Cols. 943–1210.

102 *Consultation Paper on Child Sexual Abuse*, August 1989, p. 30.

103 *Report on Child Sexual Abuse*, LRC September 1990, 32–1990.

104 Section 3 of the Protection for Persons Reporting Child Abuse Act 1998. See also Para. 1.20 of the *Report on Child Sexual Abuse*, 1990. Similar unequivocal calls for legislative reform in reporting of child abuse were made in the *Kilkenny Incest Investigation Report* (Dublin: Government Publications, 1993), p. 100, and subsequently reiterated in the *Report of the Committee of Enquiry into the Death of Kelly Fitzgerald* (Interim Report of Joint Oireachtas Committee on the Family, 1996), p. 6. As in other jurisdictions, fear of being sued for defamation tends to act as a barrier to the reporting of child abuse.

105 Section 3 (1) (a) and (b). The Act further gives protection to the *bona fide* reporter from penalisation by their employer (s. 4) and provides also for an offence in respect of false reporting of child abuse.

106 Under the Guardianship of Infants Act 1964, Section 3, 'welfare' is stated to comprise religious, moral, intellectual, physical and social welfare.

107 Article 40.3.1 of the Irish Constitution states: 'The State shall, in particular, by its laws protect as best it may from unjust attack and in the case of injustice done, vindicate the life, person, good name and property rights of every citizen.'

108 D. Glendenning, 1999, p. 443.

109 In 1996, the Irish Government issued a discussion document, *Putting Children First: A Discussion Document on Mandatory Reporting* (Dublin: Government Publications, 1996). Following a thorough consultation process the Government rejected the option of mandatory reporting as not being 'in the immediate future . . . in the best interests of children'. (Minister for Health and Children Statement, 23 December 1996.)

110 Dublin: Government Publications, September 1999.

111 C.N. McElwee, 'From Legislation to Practice: Some Observations on the 1991 Child Care Act', 4 *IJFL*, [1999] p. 8. The Working Group found that hitherto there was 'a lot of variation and a lack of consistency in the guidelines of different organisations'.

112 H. Buckley, 'Risk Assessment In Child Care Proceedings' 1 *IJFL* (2000) 6. See also *State (D and D) v. Groark* [1988] IR 187; [1990] IR 305. Also K. McGrath, 'Intervening in Child Sexual Abuse in Ireland: Towards Victim-Centred Policies and Practices', [1996]. 46 *Administration* 57. There is a Government commitment to publish a White Paper in 2000 on Mandatory Reporting of Child Abuse.

113 Statement by Junior Minister for Health and Children, 21 September 1999.

114 'Aiming for Zero Child Poverty', *Poverty Today*, March/April 2000. This issue contains thirteen incisive essays on various aspects of child poverty in Ireland.

115 ibid., p. 3. For the CPA submission to the National Children's Strategy see '*A Better Future for Children: Eliminating Poverty, Promoting Equality*'. This document is also available on the CPA website http://www.cpa.ie

116 Brian Nolan, *Child Poverty in Ireland* (Dublin: ERSI, 2000).

117 The Bill was introduced by Deputy Roisín Shorthall, who has also recently called for the establishment of a Department of Children which 'could cut through the red tape created by the current administrative structures'.

118 For a comprehensive analysis of this international child law area and the implications of incorporation see U. Kilkelly, *The Child and the European Convention on Human Rights* (Dartmouth: Ashgate, 1999).

119 H. Swindells et al. *Family Law and the Human Rights Act 1998.* (Bristol: Jordans, 1999) p. 91.

120 Freeman, supra, n. 87, at p. 61.

121 S. Toope, 'The Convention on the Rights of the Child: Implications for Canada', at pp. 44–6, in M. Freeman (ed.), *Children's Rights: A Comparative Perspective* (Darmouth, Aldershot, 1996).

122 Minister Hanafin, 'The National Children's Strategy', in *Poverty Today*, 1999, p. 8.

123 On the potential role of an Irish Children's Ombudsperson as a champion and protector of children's rights see F. Martin, 'Towards the Establishment of a Children's Ombudsman: Champion of Children's Rights or Unnecessary Interloper?' Part 1 1, *IJFL* [1998], pp. 8–21; Part 2 2, *IJFL* [1998], pp. 15–20.

124 H. Davidson, 'Applying an International Innovation to Help U.S. Children: The Child Welfare Ombudsman', 28 *Family L.Q.* (1994) 117, p. 138.

Select Bibliography

Alderson, P., *Young Children's Rights* (London: Jessica Kingsley, 2000)

Alston, A. (ed.), *The Best Interests of the Child* (Oxford: Clarendon Press, 1994)

Alston, A., Parker, S., and Seymour, J., *Children, Rights and the Law* (Oxford: Clarendon Press, 1992)

Bainham, A., and Cretney, C., *Children: The Modern Law* (Bristol: Jordans, 1998)

Beaumont, P., and McEleavy, P., *The Hague Convention and International Child Abduction* (Oxford: Oxford University Press, 1999)

Bloy, D.J., *Principles of Child Law*, 2nd edn (London: Cavendish, 1999)

Buckley, H., 'Child Abuse Guidelines in Ireland: For Whose Protection?' in Ferguson, H. and McNamara, M., *Protecting Irish Children: Investigation, Protection and Welfare* (Dublin: Institute of Public Administration, 1996)

Buckley, H., 'Protecting Children under the Child Care Act 1991 – Getting the Balance Right' (*Irish Journal of Family Law*, 1, 10, 1999)

Coggans, and Jackson, *Family Law (Divorce) Act 1996* (Dublin: Round Hall Sweet and Maxwell, 1998)

Corrigan, C., and Forde, C., *Separate Representation for Children in Ireland* (Dublin: Coolock, 1995)

Duncan, W., 'Hague Conference on Private International Law and the Children's Conventions' (*Irish Journal of Family Law*, 5, 1998)

Eekelaar, J, and Sarcevic, P., *Parenthood in Modern Society* (The Hague: Martinus Nijhoff, 1993)

Ferguson, H., and Kenny, P., *On Behalf of the Child* (Dublin: Farmar, 1995)

Ferguson, H., and McNamara, M., *Protecting Irish Children: Investigation, Protection, and Welfare* (Dublin: IPA, 1996)

Fortin, J., *Children's Rights and the Developing Law* (London: Butterworths, 1998)

Franklin, B. (ed..), *The Handbook of Children's Rights: Comparative Policy and Practice* (London: Routledge, 1995)

Freeman, M., *Children's Rights: A Comparative Perspective* (Dartmouth: Ashgate, 1996)

Glendenning, D., *Education and the Law* (Dublin: Butterworths, 1999)

Hoggett, B., *Parents and Children* 4th edn (London: Round Hall Sweet and Maxwell, 1993)

John, M. (ed.), *Children in our Charge. The Child's Right to Resources* (London: Jessica Kingsley, 1996)

Kilbourne, S., 'The Wayward Americans – Why the USA has not ratified the UNCRC' (*Child and Family Law Quarterly,* 1998, 243)

Kilkelly, U., *Small Voices: Vital Rights* (Dublin: 1997)

Kilkelly, U., *The Child and the European Convention on Human Rights* (Dartmouth: Ashgate, 1999)

Kilkelly, U., 'The Protection of Children's Rights in Ireland: Monitoring the Monitoring Process of the UNCRC' in O'Driscoll, D. (ed.), *Irish Human Rights Review 2000,* (Dublin: Round Hall Sweet and Maxwell, 2000)

McKeown, Ferguson and Rooney, *Changing Fathers* (Cork: Collins, 1998)

Martin, F., 'The Family in the Irish Constitution: Principle and Practice' in Murphy, T. and Twomey, P. (eds.), *The Evolving Constitution of Ireland* (Oxford: Hart Publishing, 1998)

Martin, F., 'Towards the establishment of a Children's Ombudsman: Champion of Children's Rights or Unnecessary Interloper?', 1 *Irish Journal of Family Law*, Part 1, 1998, pp. 8-14: 2 *IJFL*, Part 2, 1998, pp. 15-20

Martin, F., 'UN Critical of Ireland's Child Poverty Strategies', *Poverty Today*, 20, 1999

Martin, M., 'Third Party Rights of Access to and Custody of Children' 2 *The Bar Review,*1996, 39

Nestor, J., *An Introduction to Irish Family Law* (Dublin: Gill and Macmillan, 2000)

Newell, P., *Taking Children Seriously – A Proposal for a Children's Rights Commissioner* (London: Gulbenkian Foundation, 2000)

Nolan, B., *Child Poverty in Ireland* (Dublin: Economic and Social Research Institute, 2000)

Power, C., 'Children Act 1997 Comes into Force' 1 *Irish Journal of Family Law*, 22, 1999

Shatter, A. *Family Law* 4th edn (Dublin: Butterworth, 1997)

Swindells, H. et al, *Family Law and the Human Rights Act 1998* (Bristol: Jordans, 1999)

Van Bueren, G., *The International Law on the Rights of the Child* (The Hague: Martinus Nijhoff, 1995)

Walls and Bergin, *Irish Family Legislation Handbook* (Bristol: Jordans, 1999)

Ward, P., 'Children: Detention and Abortion', in Bainham, A. (ed.), *The International Survey of Family Law* (The Hague: Martinus Nijhoff, 1999)

Ward, P,. *The Child Care Act 1991* (Dublin: Round Hall Sweet and Maxwell, 1997)

Ward, P., *The Children Act 1997*, Irish Current Law Statutes Annotated (Dublin: Round Hall, Sweet and Maxwell), 1999

White, R., Carr, P. and Low, N., *The Children Act in Practice* (London: Butterworths, 1995)

Wilson, K. and James, A., *The Child Protection Handbook*, (London: 1995)

Reports and Documents

Children First: National Guidelines for the Protection and Welfare of Children (Dublin, 1999)

Concluding Observations of the UN Committee on the Rights of the Child, (1998)

Final Report of the Commission on the Family: Strengthening Families for Life (Dublin, 1998)

First National Compliance Report of Ireland (UNCRC) (Dublin, 1996)

Kilkenny Incest Investigation Report (Dublin, 1993)

Law Reform Commission Report on Child Sexual Abuse (Dublin, 1990)

Law Reform Commission Report on Family Courts (Dublin, 1996)

Law Reform Commission Report on Illegitimacy (Dublin, 1982)

Law Society of Ireland, Code of Practice Report: Family Law in Ireland (Dublin, 1995)

Putting Children First: Discussion Document on Mandatory Reporting (Dublin, 1996)

Report of the Constitution Review Group (Dublin, 1996)

Sixth Report of the Working Group on a Courts Commission (Dublin, 1999)